"We are not alone. The astronomers are wrong. The scientists are wrong. They are here, but we cannot see them because they hide. They hide… in plain sight. We are their servants, we are their slaves, we are their property… we are theirs."

— Robert Morning Sky, *The Terra Papers*

"All the rulers of the ancient world will come to rule again."

— Linda Smith, downloaded message circa 2000

"Preparations for the 1000 years of peace have begun. The people will be led beyond what they believe. The light workers and council will be meeting regularly."

— Linda Smith, downloaded message on 10/19/2017

The Kings Are Coming

a multigenerational intergalactic odyssey

LINDA MARIA SMITH

Foreword by
Richard Smith

Edited by
Michele Seaman and **Richard Smith**

The Kings are Coming – A Multigenerational Intergalactic Odyssey
Copyright © 2017 by Linda Maria Smith.

Cover art and design by Richard Smith | Design, richardsmith.co

Library of Congress Cataloging-in-Publication Data

Smith, Linda Maria, 1964 –
    The Kings are Coming – A Multigenerational Intergalactic Odyssey
    97 pages
    Includes index.
    Summary: "A combined account between mother and daughter that illuminates the multigenerational aspects of their UFO sightings and alien contact experiences as they cross over with each other in some truly amazing and original ways." – Provided by editor.
    ISBN-10: 1548661643
    ISBN-13: 978-1548661649
1. Multigenerational Experiences 2. Alien Love Bite 3. Hybrid Children
4. Extraterrestrial 5. Alien Abduction 6. Direct Alien Contact
7. Chosen Bloodlines 8. Regression Therapy 9. The Watchers
10. Galactic Community

Dedications

This book is dedicated to my family. The ones who have always been there for me, comforting me through all the ups and downs I have gone through.

My sister, Michele. You are always there for me. You never fail in your support. I know you are only a phone call away, but I treasure the times when we are together! I love you immensely! You and Tim have been extremely generous to me over the years and I feel as if I can never repay you. Thank you from the bottom of my heart. I love you both.

My parents, Ruth and Mike, who left this earth way too early. I know you are still watching over your two girls. We both love and miss you terribly! Mom, without your journal and your insistence that I also keep a record of my own experiences, this book would not exist.

My children, Robert, Melissa, Kenny and Jaclyn. My love for you is endless. You all have a special place in my heart, and I am so proud of the adults you have become. I love you, and I absolutely love the seven grandchildren I have. They put a smile on my face every single day!

To my grandparents, for always spoiling us. You always made sure we had everything we could possibly need or want.

And last, but definitely not least, Richard, the little red-haired boy of my childhood, my husband and the love of my life! I know you were sent back into my life in 2016 because we were paired as children by our ET guides and they wanted us together. You are my Knight in shining armor, the one who always goes above and beyond to make me happy. Your love brought me back from the deep dark place I was hiding in. Because of you and your love I am living again, not just existing. You fill my heart and complete me. Thank you. Without your support, guidance, love and insistence, this book would still be sitting in my drawer collecting dust!

Table of Contents

Initial Commentary

Acknowledgments

Foreword by Richard Smith

Preface by Linda Smith

Acknowledgments

To all the friends I've had over the years, thank you. You each have left an indelible mark on my heart and I will never forget you. Christine Cipolla, my very first friend who I've known since we were both five years living in Uniondale. Paula Kotoski, my other oldest friend who moved into the Uniondale neighborhood when we all were in third grade. Both of you are still my dearest friends, even more like sisters, and then there is little Lenore Linekin, my other little sister from Uniondale, my sister's best friend. Then there are my Freeport friends. Mildred Menendez, you were my very first friend in Freeport and welcomed me with open arms. I will never forget that! To my sorority sisters from Sigma Tau Delta. My neighbor Spencer Whaley. You will always be the little brother I never had.

I would also like to acknowledge some very dear friends that I still have in Freeport: Marisol Ramirez 1 & 2, Lisa Mascaro-Kropp, Beth King (RIP), Keith Young (and his children Kaley, Christian and Keira), John and Maureen Wensley (their children Lauren, Sean and Kevin) Steve and Sharon Moskowitz and the majority of the Freeport Fire Department, Wendy Kistela, Stanley Kistela, Stephanie Kistela and her little son Sean, Pamela Chila and Kenny Smith, Doreen Chila and so many more. Freeport will always be my hometown. I miss you all and thanks to social media I can still stay in contact with you.

To my new New Mexico friends, thank you for the warm welcome. Joshua Templar and his family, Mari and Corey Smith, Gloria Hawker, Larry Nasello, Brett Colin Sheppard, Karen Christine Patrick, Mary Munoz, Hannah Messoline, Andrea Atkerson, Kim Finke, Alissa Harvey, Maria Elena Rivera, Terry Kominiak, Kammie Mueller, Christine Romero, Sarah Sandoval, Kathy Rains, Amy Hurley, Paige Mann, Meg Stearns, Leah Dolan, Joanne Bahrmann, Kristin Padilla, Amy Tomlinson, Gina Foster, Noel Horcasitas, Wendy Morse, Amy Tomlinson, Colleen Carper, Ursula Kelly, Toby Chavez, Rosemary Blank and Jessica Heras. Thank you for making me feel at home from the very first day!

Foreword

Richard Smith

By the time you read this, I will have already celebrated my forty-seventh birthday. This means I am old enough to remember how things went down in the Eighties and Nineties regarding UFO sightings, alien abduction phenomena, extraterrestrial contact and the ancient astronaut theories that were just coming into public awareness at the time. I remember shallow two-dimensional talk show hosts like Phil Donahue intentionally going out of their way to crucify researchers like Budd Hopkins on daytime television. I remember two-faced backstabbing hypocrites like Carl Sagan and Phillip Klass flip-flopping on the ancient aliens scenario, all the while using their questionable status of privilege, influence and self-entitlement to deliberately misinform and disinform the general public with their Gestapo tactics. I remember Native Americans like Robert Morning Sky being chased down and severely beaten in the streets of a very white and highly racist Australia due to the highly controversial nature and gravity of his Hopi-Sumerian cosmology seminars. I remember everyone from Dr. J. Allen Hynek and Betty Hill to Erich von Däniken and Zecharia Sitchin being purposely and strategically restricted from the public dialogue of a jaded and misguided Suburban America. In truth, if it wasn't for people like Leonard Nimoy, Robert Stack and Henry Winkler, there would have been no dialogue at all to poke and prod our provincial perceptions.

Though topics like alien contact have been – and may always be – on the receiving end of social ridicule and emotional abuse, we should all remember that change is the only constant in the universe. It is that constant universal change that forces us, kicking and screaming all the way, into a more progressive state of emotional, psychological and spiritual perfection. This book serves as modern day proof of that very same change in the 21st Century for today is quite different from yesterday. Hey, don't take my word for it. Just look around you. Contactees are no longer being ostracized from their families. Abductees have support groups and meetings held in broad daylight everywhere and are no longer hiding in the closet. Conferences and seminars are promoted in abundance annually across the planet in the spirit of cooperation. Regardless of whatever scrutinizing backdraft we are still experiencing, public discussion is at an all-time high, penetrating the political, economic and professional bandwidths of our global society.

Local communities now openly embrace such metaphysical dialogue in the modern world. Yes, it can definitely be said that things have changed for the better and in a big way. In a sense, the establishment's witch burnings have ceased, receding into the shadows of whatever backwards superstitious dementia they came from. And, with international discussion and research trending towards a more open and sincere candidness, I think it's fair to say that terms like paranormal, metaphysical and supernatural will soon be given a more accepting and down to earth understanding of what has always been the normal, physical and natural mysteries of lost knowledge, ancient wisdom and the modern world we live in. Ultimately, that which we have been experiencing as magick amounts to nothing more than a higher form of science without a text book in our esoteric origins of humanity. Things are coming full circle in our world as we openly revisit and vigorously embrace what we have tragically lost from the past, our roots. Our interstellar roots, to be exact, which includes our star born alien legacy among the stars.

That being said, now is time to bring about great change in the world for the betterment of humanity's psychological progress and emotional growth. Now is the time for embracing the reality of a much larger galactic community, an infamous truth that has always existed in the backdrop of human evolution on the fringes of our global society – extraterrestrial intervention and direct alien contact with the people of Earth. "The Kings Are Coming" represents not only a major global sea change for the common layman's worldview but an admission of truth on the personal level as well. Author Linda Smith stands witness to an extraterrestrial reality spanning at least four generations in her family, something that would cause most to crack up, sit in a padded room or run for the hills. It is the kind of book that would have been guaranteed a glorious bonfire burning in Ray Bradbury's "Fahrenheit 451" reality that existed in the 20th Century. Yet, as my good friend Ruth would say, "patience… things happen for a reason when they are supposed to happen."

On that note, thank goodness "The Kings Are Coming" is being published for the first time, here and now, and just in time for the grand awakening we are all going through presently and will continue to experience in the years to come. The author herself has gone through quite a few emotional and familial hurdles to get to this point in her life, to feel emboldened enough to get her experiences out there while inspiring many others to come forward and speak out about their experiences as well. Once again, it goes back to that great change in perception and social awareness that has given the subject of alien contact the ability to be welcomed with open arms on a spiritual, communal and international level, thus paving the way for a brave, powerful and inspirational book like "The Kings Are Coming" to ever exist at all. The author writes it in such a manner making it very hard to peel yourself away from its highly revealing day-by-day journaled format, a combined account between mother and daughter that illuminates the multigenerational aspects of their UFO sightings and alien contact experiences as they cross over with each other in some truly amazing and original ways. One such experience delves into the shocking revelation of a lifelong alien love bite scenario between Linda and her husband while another centers around an astounding admission regarding the birth of hybrid human-alien female twins, the biological offspring that came directly from that very same bonded love bite coupling mentioned above. As it turns out, one of those female twins was allowed to stay here on Earth and be raised by her human parents from birth to adulthood while the other has remained with her alien guardians. Yes, you must read the book.

As you can see, this kind of thing runs in the family and is more common than we realize or care to admit to in terms of ancient human bloodlines throughout the modern-day world – yours, mine and the next-door neighbor's. As this book implies, we all have Elders in the stars of the galactic community watching over us since time immemorial. As this book shows, we have never ever been alone in this world.

– Richard Smith
December 2017

Richard Smith is a professional life-changing speaker, experiencer, web design consultant and author on the topic of extraterrestrial contact, the Moorish Legacy, human origins and related matters. Smith received high honors at New York State University for his work with extraterrestrial intervention and alien contact phenomena. An author of two books, "The Moor, The Mason and The Alien: A Call to Action" and "Legions of Light / Armies of Darkness," Smith is committed to raising conscious awareness in our health and well-being as caretakers of the planet as well as creating a better understanding of our place in the Cosmos. For more information, visit ufoteacher.com today.

Preface

Linda Maria Smith

The story you are about to read is my story. A long and twisted story of my extraterrestrial escapades that began in 1967. It is full of threads of information that were painstakingly pieced together from many broken memories. I'm hoping that one day those gaps will be filled to make my memories complete. It is not easy to speak about these experiences with the general public because even I cannot comprehend some of the memories I have. It is only recently that I have started speaking publicly with a local group of people who understand or want to understand the UFO phenomenon.

Brian Levens from LIUFON suggested I try regression therapy to try to trigger my memories. My first regression therapy session was back in 1996 with Dr. Jean Mundy, but not much came out of that session. In September 2017, I started working with a local hypnotherapist who worked with Bud Hopkins in the past. Her name is Gloria Hawker and she is helping me unlock the suppressed memories in my mind with hopes that I can start remembering all that I have stored away over the years. The first session I had with her was a success. I was able to remember an experience that was not mentioned in either my or my mother's journal. The memory was with me on a ship in some sort of medical room. I was sitting on a very futuristic-looking chair with a metallic headband with copper circular discs on my temples. There was an ET in the room with me and it was working on some machine that resembled an MRI machine or some form of diagnostic machine. The ET was long and slender with a large bulbous head and his clothing was the same color as its skin, a mottled brownish color. The headband I was wearing was putting a lot of pressure on my temples and was giving me a headache. I was wearing some sort of white shimmering jumpsuit while sitting in this chair and, somehow, I just knew I was being prepared for something. [drawing, fig. 13]

I do not claim to be an expert on anything relating to the paranormal or extraterrestrial. This book is solely based on my experiences including my mother's, my sister's and other family members' experiences spanning a timeframe from 1967 to 2017. I am still having experiences here in New Mexico.

My very first memory of seeing anything out of the ordinary was at the age of three when I found myself face to face with two small beings standing in the hallway in front of my mother's bedroom door. From 1967 to 1979, I had what seemed like nightly experiences with ET visitors. To my recollection I never had a horrifying experience but that could just be an implanted memory. What I have come to realize through meditation and piecing together my fragmented memories is that I am a key player in a multi-generational extraterrestrial experience for the past fifty years. My nightly paranormal visits are for some sort of training and prepping for what is to come in the very near future. I also have been given downloaded information in bits and pieces over the past thirty years, most of which does not make any sense to me. I am not well versed in any UFO literature like my mother was and I am not able to throw out names of famous UFO investigators or authors like everyone else. However, the messages I received and spoke during my downloaded sessions would make perfect sense to my mother as she would write everything down and then go through her library of books to validate my statements. She would then write everything down in her journal including what she was able to validate from her books.

I have been asked on several occasions recently how many alien species have I seen over the years and my reply is always the same. I have seen many different species over the past fifty years. This is because I was a participant in an alien classroom aboard a ship during my childhood. I was learning from each of the many different alien species in the classroom as well as the Elders who were there to guide and prepare us for the future tasks we were chosen for. The Elders are the extraterrestrial beings I have had numerous encounters with over my lifetime. I also call them the Watchers. They are a gentle and loving race and have been an extremely important part of my life, telepathically guiding me and teaching me since childhood. They are human-like beings with an appearance very similar to ours except for their large eyes and large head. Their clothing resembles a shimmering white robe with a symbol just below their left shoulder that I now know as the Merkabah Star Tetrahedron. The small ETs that I saw when I was three years old are the ones I refer to as the Kings. It was a term my sister came up with when we were very young and to this day we do not know why she chose that term. I believe that these small beings work very closely with the Elders.

I started putting this book together in 2013 but I never finished it because it was difficult to sort through all of my mother's notes. It wasn't until 2016 when my husband, Richard, convinced me to get my book out there and share my story so that those who have had similar life experiences are not afraid to come forward and talk openly about their experiences. He has been my driving force to finish what I started. So, Richard, I thank you from the bottom of my heart. Since 1995 you have been my friend, my support, my confidant and my love. I am so happy that we are finally together, married and free to show our love for each other. I love you with every fiber of my being.

You are my immortal beloved and I will love you forever!

– Linda Smith
  November 2017

CHAPTER ONE

The Kings Are Coming

When I was very young I hated the dark and I did not like being alone in my bedroom at night. I would wake up almost every night in a panic because I felt as if I had just fallen back into my bed. On many occasions I would walk into my parents' room next door and crawl into bed next to my mother. That is where I felt safe.

My earliest memory of what I can now call an alien encounter was when I was three years old in 1967. On this particular night, I woke up as usual feeling as if I had fallen back into bed. I got out of bed and walked into the hallway towards my parents' bedroom but something was in my way. I remember hearing a strange sound and noticed what I thought initially was the dog standing in front of me. It was completely dark yet I could see four small feet glowing with a whitish blue luminescence. I looked up to see two small beings staring at me just as I heard "go back to bed" in my head. So, I did just that, which was not what I would normally do. These beings were not much taller than me and they appeared to be glowing in the dark. To this day I'm still not sure if they were there for me or for my mother who was pregnant with my sister. Maybe they were there for both of us. I have no further memory of anything else happening after returning to my bed that night.

My sister, Michele, was born in January of 1968 just before my fourth birthday. We shared that room next to my parents' bedroom until we were old enough, in my parents' eyes, to move upstairs to one of the two spare bedrooms. I think Michele and I moved to the upstairs bedroom when I was ten and she was six years old. The two bedrooms upstairs were identical in size and they each had double walk-in closets that were huge with one window between the closets. Our bedroom was light and bright with white paneling and a white linoleum floor that looked like marble. In my opinion, the other room was dark and gloomy. It had dark hardwood flooring, dark wood molding and big heavy dark wood

8

furniture. This was the room my father's parents stayed in when they came to visit on the weekends from Jackson Heights, Queens.

My father and his parents came from Cuba in 1957 and lived in Queens, New York. My Cuban grandmother lovingly called our house in Uniondale the beach house not because we were on the beach but because it was very close to Jones Beach, compared to Jackson Heights, and we would go out on our boat to spend the day on the beach during the summer.

The room my Cuban grandparents would stay in during their weekend visits terrified my sister and I, especially if the door was open and no one was upstairs. There was always a creepy feeling emanating from that room and we would only go up there when we had to. It was rare for us to have friends up in our room to play. We either played outside, at our friends' homes or downstairs in the living room. If the door to my grandparents' room were open when either my sister or I went upstairs, we would run really fast into our bedroom and totally avoid looking into the other bedroom. Our bedroom door faced the other room and there was a small bathroom in between. I remember that we dreaded going to bed at night because it meant that we would be alone up there. The dark room across the hall was where these beings came from. At least, that is what we thought. I remember saying to my sister "the Kings are coming" and we would scream and pull the blankets up to our faces in fear of what would happen at night. They were a small alien species that would take us to a ship during the night.

My sister's first recollection of an experience takes place just after seeing a very bright light come from the bathroom window when she was about six or seven years old. Afterwards, having been traumatized by some type of experience in the upstairs bathroom, she remembers sitting at the top of the stairs calling out for our mother. She told me she remembers sitting at the top step after this incident and was yelling "mommy, mommy, mommy" but no sound was coming out of her mouth. All my sister will say is that "they did something to me that night" but cannot recall the actual experience or has completely blocked it from her memory, refusing to even attempt to remember. She also remembers one other experience while sleeping in the dark spare room one night with our grandfather. She said she opened her eyes to see a shadowy figure sitting above her on the headboard of the bed. She told me, "it was the man." To this day my sister insists she has no other memories of aliens or abductions but my mother's journal proves otherwise. My poor sister has repressed her memories of those strange nights. We hated sleeping upstairs.

During the summer of 1976, just before I started attending Turtle Hook junior high school, my parents thought it would be a brilliant idea to give us our own rooms. Guess where I was sleeping now. Yes, the dreaded dark room! Just great. I figured I'd better start facing whatever is in that damned room. So, after painting my room blue one afternoon (don't ask), I decided to open both of those wretched closets and take a look inside. I went into the one closest to the bedroom door first. I looked around and sat on one of my grandmother's suitcases. After being there for a moment, that creepy feeling started in my gut. I said to myself, "no one is here Linda, it's broad daylight and mom is right downstairs. Nothing is going to happen." I started looking through the stuff that was there, all of which amounted to nothing more than some of my grandmother's clothing, pictures and more suitcases. There was nothing to worry about. Yet, I still had this strange feeling in the pit of my stomach that I was being watched. The other closet was filled with my grandfather's clothes, his 8mm movie projector, some reels of old home movies from Cuba, a slide projector and boxes of slides. All in all, just a normal set of closets. However, when it came time for bed, that room transformed into a portal and I never knew what to expect.

The fear of being visited or taken started to change shortly after I was in my new room. I wasn't paralyzed by fear anymore. The experiences were now about learning. I have several memories of being in a room with other children of varying ages – almost like a school – but the "children" in that classroom were not all human. It was becoming a familiar place for me during my extraterrestrial travels. There were several experiences during the time period of 1976 that included me being with a younger red-haired boy. We seemed to be very close even though he was much younger. I don't remember exactly when he started showing up in my experiences, but I believe I was close to ten or eleven years old. We were together until I was about fifteen years of age. The children in that classroom setting were my friends but this little red-haired boy was extra special and I know I was assigned to watch over him and to protect him at all costs. Most of the memories I have of my classroom experiences are murky. They are choppy and it is almost like watching a slide show rather than a movie. All that aside, there is one memory in particular that is quite clear. The little red-haired boy and I are on the ship, as we always are, holding hands and walking towards the classroom. I believe I had just picked him up from the part of the ship where the arrivals were held and was taking him to the classroom when we were stopped in the middle of this dimly lit corridor. A being suddenly grabbed him and started pulling him away from me. I turned towards the being that was doing this with a look of confusion that said, "Why are you taking him away from me?" The little boy was screaming while he was trying to hang on to my arm as he was being hauled away. I'm not sure how old he was in this memory, but I would guess he's about six or seven. I remember not being very happy about having my special friend yanked away from me and I don't remember getting any explanation as to why they took him away either. I do remember looking down towards a door that was slightly opened and could see that there were several beings in a room that resembled a conference room of sorts. There were at least two beings standing together as if they were conferring with each other and they looked my way when the little red-haired boy was taken from me. I was approached by another being and led into that open door. I was able to get a good look at this huge room now. It was an open space with theater type seating. There were several beings sitting in the seats and a few standing as well. I was led towards the group that was standing. There was a familiarity that came over me as I got closer to the beings. I cannot remember why I was there, but I have a strong knowing that I was part of that meeting.

In 1979, I had just started my sophomore year at Uniondale High School when we moved from Uniondale to Freeport. This was an exciting time for Michele and I. In my mind, I was going to be able to start fresh in a new school. I wasn't very popular in Uniondale. I wasn't part of the cool crowd and I was made fun of by some classmates in school and on the bus. During this period of my life, I openly discussed certain beliefs about other life forms on other planets. I was very fascinated by the stars at night and always felt as if I didn't belong here on this planet. Needless to say, I was teased about it, which forced me to keep quiet about my experiences, even to my mother. So, moving to a new town was the beginning of a fresh start for me or so I thought. Not much in the way of any experiences happened during our move. At least, I have no recollection of any as there seemed to be a period of time where nothing happened to my sister or me. However, it could just be that I have suppressed these memories. What I do remember is that I had a heightened sense of sexuality during my early teen years. I didn't act upon anything, but I do remember being on a ship where I was being watched and/or guided to perform some sexual acts with a younger boy. Yes, the red-haired boy that was younger than me. When I was sixteen, I lost my virginity to my first boyfriend, Louie. It wasn't anything to write home about. It didn't feel right. I almost felt as if I was searching for something or someone here, but I couldn't put my finger on it. Fifteen years would go by before any new recollections of experiences would come flooding into my memory.

In 1982, I graduated from high school. In 1987, I gave birth to my first child and, in 1989, I got married for the first time. In 1994, my mother started attending a book club in Massapequa, the same year my mother started recording her UFO sightings. I'm not sure exactly what prompted her to start recording her sightings, but I think something was triggered for her with the new group she was meeting with. She would sit at the kitchen window in our Freeport house and record every strange set of lights in the sky over the canals. My mother and I started discussing her sightings one night and this gave me an opportunity to finally open up to her about what Michele and I had experienced in Uniondale. This was the beginning of a whole new set of experiences for us.

My mother and I attended a few Star People meetings together. She introduced me to Joanne and Janet, both of whom are local Long Island psychics and the originators of Star People. I also met a few other key people in this group, one of whom was Brian Levens. He was the senior investigator for LIUFON and was very interested in our experiences. By December of 1995, my mother had documented an extensive list of sightings and experiences in her notebook. My mother was introduced to another group who were into the UFO phenomenon, a Long Island organization called "The Eyes of Learning." She was starting to realize that she was not the only one seeing these lights and it was sort of a confirmation for her that what she was seeing and experiencing was real. My mother met a new member to Star People around this time. He was a young local artist and was very knowledgeable on the topic of UFOs. He was having an art gallery reception at SUNY Old Westbury on December 11, 1995, and had invited the entire group to attend his art exhibition.

By this time, I was at the end of my pregnancy with my third child and getting settled in my new home. My ex-husband Ken and I bought our first home and closed on the house just before Christmas that year. I will explain in detail in another chapter about this pregnancy and all the experiences that surrounded it, starting in 1994.

Through in-depth conversations with my mother and others over the years, and my mother's insistence that I meditate, I have been able to piece together memories of my experiences. I have memories of being around a praying mantis-like creature and having some heated arguments with this being. I recall staring up at this massive fifteen-foot-tall being while shaking my fist at her, asking her why she will not let me remember. I have memories of being a member of an interstellar group called The Sisterhood, an ET council comprised of members of several different species of alien races, including the human race, all working together. As a member of this ET council, I now know why I was escorted into the room when I was younger to be a part of that gathering in the memory I described earlier. The Crone, or Mother (the large mantis being) is the head of this ET council and, for some reason, has taken me under her wing as her protégé since I was a child. The Elders work very closely with the Crone and have also been guiding me throughout my life. The Kings that used to come and take my sister and I at night are a group of ETs from what I believe is the Zeta Reticuli race. They work very closely with the Crone and the Sisterhood and are the ones that brought us aboard the ship where the Crone and the Elders were, the same ship where my sister and I were taught things beyond human comprehension.

There is one significant memory I have from 1996 when I was being taught how to fly a craft. I clearly remember learning how to telepathically control the ship while gently touching the symbols on the flat glass control panel. I knew exactly what each symbol meant and which ones to touch so as to maneuver the craft. What blew my mind was that I was being taught how to fly this spacecraft! I drew a picture of what I saw and have included it in this book. [drawing, fig. 1]

Over the years, I have been trained how to heal using heat energy from my hands to ease any discomfort someone may have such as a headache or tight muscles. I have also been trained to be in tune with my intuition and have finely tuned my empathic abilities, feeling other people's emotions. Being in a room with many people is sometimes difficult for me. I can feel the emotions from everyone at once and it can be quite overwhelming at times. The term empath was not known to me back when I was a child but has become a very popular term in recent years. My sister is also an empath as she is able to feel the pain of others. I am certain that if my sister and I were put into a situation that required us to use our empathic abilities we would be quite a team.

CHAPTER TWO
The Book Of Ruth

My mother, Ruth, was always a quiet and somewhat shy person. She was never one to go out with her friends and she never had a job until my sister was in middle school and I was in high school. Even then she only worked part time and was always home before we got home from school. My mother never really showed any interest in any outside activities apart from doing stage makeup for a local theater group and for the Uniondale High School drama club while we were growing up. It wasn't until 1994 that she started showing an interest in a group called Star People. I don't remember how she found this group.

I went to a few of the book club meetings with my mother and I met her friends, Joanne and Janet, the group's originators and local Long Island psychics. Brian was the senior investigator for LIUFON and there were a few other members. It was during one of the first meetings I attended that I realized the book club was about paranormal and extraterrestrial topics. My mother started bringing home books by Zecharia Sitchin, Erich von Däniken and Edgar Cayce just to name a few and her interest exploded into a frenzy of digesting every book she could get her hands on relating to UFOs and alien abductions. It was as if something clicked and things were starting to make sense for her. She was constantly reading, researching and comparing notes. Her favorite book was "Beyond My Wildest Dreams" by Kim Carlsberg.

The end of December, 1994, was when my mother started documenting her sightings in what I now call "The Book of Ruth." She would sit at the kitchen table and look out the huge bow window every night. I remember her saying that she felt compelled to go to the window or to go outside. Every time she did she would have a sighting and document it. It was as if they were calling her outside. Some nights I would sit there with her and there were a few nights that we both had sightings. Her book spans the timeframe of 1994 through 2001 and is extremely detailed.

My mother's health started to decline in 2001 after her first heart attack. She went on to survive three major heart operations and eventually passed away on August 25, 2005, from a cerebral hemorrhage. I sat with her in the hospital room all alone for quite some time holding her hand in disbelief that my mother was in a coma. A piece of me died that day. This book is dedicated to her because she was my guide and mentor on this journey. My mother and I created a deep bond during the eleven years from 1994 to 2005 and were able to share our sightings and experiences with each other.

A special dedication for my mother Ruth (aka: Turtle)

We shared eleven glorious years documenting our UFO experiences, forging a bond I never could imagine. Together, we were a team in an intergalactic odyssey experiencing things one only reads about in science fiction books.

Thank you for urging me to start writing down my experiences and thank you for keeping such detailed notes of your own experiences. Without these two journals, this book would not exist. This book is dedicated to you. Since your passing in 2005, I have been terribly lost without you and still suffer from depression. How I managed to take care of my children without you is beyond me. You would be so proud of the adults they have grown up to be and you'd be so happy to be around my seven grandchildren. There is not a day that goes by that I don't think about you and it still makes me cry. I feel your presence and can still hear your voice. I would give anything to talk to you and hug you once again.

I miss you terribly! I wish I could call you just one more time to hear your voice and your laugh.

I will love you forever…

With love from your oldest daughter,

Linda (Ria)

The following chapters represent our documented sightings and experiences along with scanned photos of my markings and drawings of experiences throughout the years. You will see that there are some dates that match each other's journal entries. I found it very interesting as I was writing this book.

CHAPTER THREE
1994 - 1995

December, 1994, was when my mother first started writing down her sightings. I'm sure there were many sightings or experiences prior to this but for some reason this is when she decided to start documenting them. Things progressed quite rapidly from this point on.

A few of our close neighbors told my mother that they also witnessed what she had documented in the earlier part of 1995. We lived in the south part of Freeport on waterfront property so every house in our neighborhood had a canal in their backyard. The activity my mother was witnessing took place mostly over the canal across the street from us (south side of the block) or over the open water at the cul de sac on our street. All of our entries and experiences will be in date order starting with 1994. I will be following both journals exactly as they are entered. I have scanned pictures showing my markings and drawings I made over the years.

My mother's journal entries will be in italic and my entries will be in regular font. My mother's notes will be entered exactly as they were in the original journal since she is no longer alive to elaborate. I will explain as much as I can remember for my journal entries. Okay, ready? Here we go:

#1) *(I had just gotten up – went immed. to kitchen and sat down) Last week of 12/94 at 5:58 AM – Triangular (LARGE) craft "popped up" from behind neighbor's house, and headed east over rooftops to the end of the street, then turned right and went south over the water. Craft was moving very slowly, and silently. Lights on craft were quite visible since it was still dark outside. Est. size of craft, front to back was 40 – 60 ft.*

#2) *Sun., 2-12-95 at 6:02 AM – Same type of triangular craft appeared again, silently over rooftops across the street, heading west.*

#3) *Sun., 2-12-95 at 8:45 PM – Neighbor Debbie (across the street) heard strange noise outside, looked out back window and saw same type of Tri. Craft hovering over canal, heading west (directly behind her house)*

Debbie was my friend and our neighbor about four houses down from us across the street. Our kids would play together all the time. She told my mother what she witnessed in the early evening of 2/12/95 at approximately 8:45 p.m. My mother had seen the same craft earlier that day at approximately 6:02 a.m. Debbie told my mother that she heard a strange humming coming from the backyard so she went to look out onto the upper deck to see where the noise was coming from when she saw a large triangular craft hovering over the canal directly in front of her. She said she watched it float down the canal toward S. Main Street, which was towards the west. She was so shaken by her encounter that she never spoke of it again. She moved away a few months later. I went to visit her at her new place in Seaford once, we discussed the sighting one more time and then we never heard from her again.

#4) *Tues., 2-14-95 at 5:48 AM – Linda saw a "dome-shaped light" visible at chimney level behind the houses across the street, starting from the eastern end of the block, moving at a slow steady pace, heading westbound until the light suddenly blinked off at the western end of the block at 5:56 AM – sighting lasted 8 minutes. No sounds.*

#5) *Sun., 2-19-95 at 12:08 AM – Low flying, silent craft came in from the east, moving somewhat faster, turned left over neighbor's house, directly across the street and headed south towards the park.*

#6) *Tues., 3-21-95 at 9:50 PM – Linda and Lisa (possible cigar or cylindrical shaped) Saw different type craft, with different lighting, over houses at east end of street; it went from a horizontal position to vertical then took off and disappeared.*

My first entry into my journal was on March 21, 1995. During this time I was a manicurist/nail technician and I ran the business out of my mother's house since 1992. My clients would sometimes have to make an appointment in the evening and I was able to accommodate them because I worked at home. Most of my nail clients had been with me since 1992 and had become more than just clients they were close friends. Denise and Heidi were two of my long-time clients that became very close friends of mine.

On Thursday evenings their appointments were back to back and we would have a blast while I did their nails. We would watch television or listen to music and talk about our lives. We even started having "margarita nights". They were so much fun to be with! I still communicate with them through Facebook.

Lisa, was another one of my regular nail clients. She and her mother would come together every two weeks to get their nails done at my house. On this one particular night Lisa came alone. It was about 9:50 pm when I finished painting her nails. (as part of my nail service, I always helped my clients open the car door, turn on the car for them and buckle their seat belt for them so they wouldn't mess up their nails.) As Lisa and I were walking up to her car, I noticed four lights up in the sky out of the corner of my eye. They were just at the end of my block to my left. I asked Lisa to look also just to make sure I wasn't seeing things. There were two large white lights at each end and two smaller red lights in the middle. I couldn't see any visible structure, just the lights. They were floating directly above the house not up high in the sky like a star cluster. As we walked closer to the end of the block to get a better look I watched as the lights flipped from horizontal to vertical and started pulsing one after another like a strobe light. Slow at first then it picked up speed. Then in a flash it took off straight up into the night sky. Poof! Gone.... Lisa and I walked back to her car in total amazement at what we had just witnessed. I buckled her seatbelt, started her car and said good night to her. She never returned to get her nails done again. Even after several attempts to contact her. Her mother came back a few times and mentioned Lisa was freaked out by what she saw. Then I never saw her mother again after that.

#7) *Fri., 3-24-95 at 10:40 PM – Linda and I saw a silent, well-lit craft suddenly appear from the west, at tree-top level, fly over canal behind houses across the street; craft made a sudden sharp right turn at middle of block, directly in front of us, and headed south towards Cow Meadow park – flying just high enough to clear tree tops and power lines; rear of craft visible for approx. 30 seconds after turning south.*

On 4/11/95, my mother invited a new member, James Lefante, from her UFO group over to discuss his UFO experiences. I sat with them in the kitchen for a while and listened. Around 11:00pm I was tired, so I excused myself to go to bed. James got up and said he had to leave also because it was getting late. He walked out the door as I was heading downstairs. I brushed my teeth and then went to my bedroom where my husband was already fast asleep.

As I lay there in the dark just starting to fall asleep I started getting this strange tingly sensation all over me. I started to feel heavy as if some invisible force was holding me down. I was aware of my body but I couldn't move at all. I thought to myself, "What the hell is going on?" I opened my eyes but the room was too dark to see anything. Then it all went blank. I told my mother about this experience the next morning. About a six weeks later I found out I was pregnant. I went to see my doctor for an exam and blood work to confirm my pregnancy. The doctor pulled out his little wheel they used back then to determine a due date. Based on his calculations my due date was 1/18/96. According to his wheel, my conception date was on or around 4/11/95. Really? What happened that night? Let me be clear about something I am not saying James had anything to do with this at all.

About twelve to fourteen weeks into my pregnancy I started cramping while I was at work. I went to the bathroom and noticed that I had blood on my underwear. I immediately went back to my desk called my doctor then told my boss and then went straight to the doctor's office. After his examination, he had me go into his office so he could talk to me. He came in and told me that although I was still pregnant, he felt that I had lost a twin. I was put on bed rest for three weeks. Twin...? Holy shit!

#8) *Fri., 6-9-95 at 10:25 PM – Saw reflection of flashing lights on open bathroom window (also heard slight sound – strobes), stepped into bathtub, looked out window to NW, saw craft flying at tree top level; could only see very bright, strong strobe lights, one on either end of craft, with a red flashing light on bottom, in center; it continued NW to WGBB radio tower then turned at level of flashing red lights on the lower portion of tower (approx. 50-75 ft. above ground) and headed west.*

#9) *Tues., 6-20-95 at 10:10 PM – Went out onto back porch (almost felt "compelled"), turned right facing east, and saw identically lit craft at treetop level heading east BEHIND MY NEIGHBOR'S HOUSES, BETWEEN THE HOUSE AND THE CANAL DIRECTLY IN BACK, flying approx. 200 ft. in front of me, when it suddenly accelerated, turned upward, almost (see below) vertical, and took off with a VERY LOUD burst of noise, went up into clouds and disappeared.*

It had been silent until it took off with a ROAR.

**Summer of 1995 (no date in journal) BLUE FLASH INCIDENT – Grandchildren had a friend sleep over one evening. They were still awake, in bed, when the friend suddenly noticed a bright blue flash in the

sky overhead…the other two boys and Linda all saw them (at my house)

Another evening, I saw bright medium blue flashed behind my neighbor's house across the street over the canal (it seemed). The flash lit up a large area; seconds later, another flash a little further east.

There were at least three more flashes, each one a little further east than the last, as if something was moving slowly over the canal towards the east end of the canal.

#10) *Fri., 11-17-95 at 10:15 PM – Linda and I saw craft over rooftops of houses across the street, heading west. Blinking set of lights – red, green, blue in middle of craft; solid white lights – one on either end. (SEE COMMENTS BELOW) NO SOUND! (only sighting with this type of sighting)*

#11) *Sun., 12-10-95 at 5:05 PM – From back door, saw triangular craft flying at treetop level, silently, heading NW towards tower – it turned left at tower again and headed west, as before. (Just before sunset; had slightly better view of craft, not just lights.) Craft was situated over the industrial park, just north of my house.*

On 12/11/95, my mother asked if I wanted to go with her to SUNY Old Westbury to go see an art exhibition that was being presented by the newest member of the Star People group. The new member Rick had invited the entire group to his event. It was a cold winter evening and I was wearing a leather jacket with a fur collar and a sweater dress with a foil print of Cleopatra on it. I remember this vividly because I will never forget this night ever! We walked into this huge warehouse-looking room to see a large display of art on several levels. I remember seeing a bunch of what looked like copper pages strewn all over the floor and a large group of people talking to each other in a huddle.

The rest is a bit fuzzy because my life changed dramatically at this point. My mother noticed that Joanne was standing near the group that was in the huddle talking when I heard my mother say, "That must be him…" We walked over to the group and I looked up to see this very tall red-haired man standing in front of me. "Hi, I'm Rick." At that moment our eyes locked and I instantly knew it was him! There he was, Richard Smith, the artist whose work I came to see.

My heart skipped a beat my stomach dropped and I had goosebumps.

There was a strange electricity buzzing between us. We said hello to each other as he reached out to shake my hand but I can't remember if anything else was said. Time seemed to stop at this point. It felt like we were staring at each other for hours without saying a word to each other. I do believe he felt the same electricity between us as I did. My mother noticed our body language but never said anything. That night was the beginning of an extraordinary chain of events. Not much happened after that and the next thing I remember is leaving with my mother to go home. From that night on I could not get this man out of my head. Everything changed for me. Everything seemed different for me in my life after meeting him. There was a strong urge to see him again and I would go to great lengths to find a way to see him.

My mother and I had become very close during these UFO experiences that had started exactly one year earlier. My mother shared with me that she believed she had been having experiences since she was a child and she also confessed that her mother may have had many UFO experiences as well. Apparently, my grandmother had an unexplained scoop mark on her shin since she was a child and could not explain where it came from. The only thing she said was that it probably came from falling off her bicycle. After doing some book research my mother found several accounts of other people having an unexplained scoop mark on their shin and they also said it was from a bicycle accident as a child. Coincidence? I think not.

#12) *Tues., 1-30-95 at 10:30 PM – At Dairy Barn on Atlantic Ave., looked up to my right (SW), saw craft flying low over stores heading NW (Location is about three blocks west of tower) Same as others – silent with typical lighting.*

COMMENTS RE: #10 (Fri. 11-17-95) About 11:30 PM I suddenly had a lout high-pitched ringing noise emanating from my left ear (similar to microphone "feedback" (?) – seemed mechanical not physical – lasted approx. 5 minutes.

Sat., 11-18-95, approx. 4:00 AM – Michele had a nightmare, felt as if she "fell back into bed," woke up crying hysterically; then noticed a small needle puncture mark on inside of right wrist (with a tiny bit of skin pulled away from mark) I saw it too.

Fri., 11-24-95 (Ken's birthday) approx. 8:00 AM – Linda woke up with tongue hurting – found a small needle puncture mark on MIDDLE of tongue (looked just like Michele's wrist) I saw it too. (See "Beyond My Wildest Dreams" by Kim Carlsberg pg. 120) (She was pregnant with Jackie)

Re: #9 – This same type of noise has been heard almost on a daily basis since then, except in times of extremely bad winter weather. One day, last summer ('95), the reverberations were so loud (and close) that rain fell for a couple of minutes. It sounded much louder than any plane – as if something were "taking off" from a nearby location. Several people have heard this, but no sightings have been associated with it.

CHAPTER FOUR

1996

January 7, 1996, was a Sunday and I had a full schedule of clients coming that day because the next day I was going to the hospital for my scheduled C-section. At around 10:00 am the snow started to fall and by noon it had gotten considerably heavier. I started to panic because the streets were covered with snow and the visibility was really poor. I called the hospital and asked if I could go in later that day due to the blizzard. The nurse on the phone said yes but I should check with my insurance company. I called my insurance company but couldn't get through. A recorded message was all I got stating that due to the weather the offices were closed. Great, now what? So, I cancelled the afternoon clients and decided to go to the hospital anyway. We left at about 3:50 PM and by the time I got to the hospital it was 5:30 in the afternoon and the snow was thick. It took us over an hour to get to the hospital when on a clear day would normally be 20 minutes. I was admitted and put in a private hospital room. Later on that night, I heard the nurses talking at the nurse's station. They were discussing who would take first shift for sleep. Right after that a doctor walked into my room, realized I wasn't the patient he was looking for and started back out of the room when I said, "Dr. Plotkin?" He turned back towards me and said, "Yes." I said, "Hi, it's me, Linda. I used to work for you in Massapequa a few years ago." I'm not sure if he really remembered me or was just being polite but he replied, "Oh, yes. Hi, how are you?" We shared some small talk and he left. The rest of the night was very quiet until about 1:00 AM and I heard sirens on and off for a while. My C-section was scheduled for 8:00 a.m. The next morning a nurse walked in around 7:45 a.m. and told me that they had had several emergency deliveries come throughout the night due to the storm and my surgery was going to be pushed back. "You know crazy weather brings babies," she said as she walked out of the room.

January 8, 1996 – 11:50 AM – Jaclyn Michele was born. On January 11, 1996 I brought her home. Eleven seems to be a recurring number in my life. Remember I mentioned earlier that I possibly conceived her on 4/11/95 per my obstetrician?

Number eleven is popping up everywhere and it started many years ago in 1993 when my mother suggested that I start meditating. During my first attempt at meditation I went outside and sat on the lawn and proceeded to meditate the way I had been told how to do it. Deep breaths and a humming sound… "Om." The darkness I saw with my eyes closed slowly turned into a very bright white room. I didn't see anything or anyone in this room, but I somehow knew it was a round room and then I heard "on the 11th day" in a deep rumbling male voice. There was no one else there with me. At least I couldn't see anyone. That comment scared the shit out of me and I quickly snapped out of my meditative state and ran back into the house to tell my mother what had just happened. Since then the number eleven has shown up everywhere. Whether it's the amount I have to pay or the change I get back from a purchase, the time on the clock (11:11) or the date of an event, it was everywhere, so much so that even my mother started commenting about it. My conception date 4/11, met Rick 12/11, brought Jaclyn home 1/11 and the 11 years (1994-2001) of documented UFO sightings and experiences I had with my mother before she passed away. It still happens to me to this day. What does it all mean? Is there some sort of message that I am not picking up on? *Side note, 2018 adds up to 11 so I know it will be a big year!

2/96 (exact date not written down) – was the first time I vividly recall having an extraterrestrial experience since 4/11/95 when I conceived my daughter. This experience was the first time I can recall actually communicating with an alien being and I was with my mother. My mother and I were sitting in a plain non-descript room. It was a very open room that felt cold and sterile. I couldn't see anyone around me but I just knew we were not alone. An Elder was walking towards me holding a baby. This baby was a bit smaller than Jaclyn and a bit frail looking but resembled my daughter. Was this the twin that I had supposedly lost? The Elder looked directly into my eyes and I heard it speak to me telepathically. It was a clear-cut message for me regarding my babies. The Elder let me hold her for a while. She looked up at me and smiled as if she knew I was her mother. When I opened my eyes, I was back in my room lying on my bed.

This was too crazy, I had to write it all down and document

everything. I know I sound crazy. Believe me I was starting to think I was crazy too. Here I am 31 years old, married with three children and I have a twin daughter up in space being taken care of by aliens. What the hell is going on?

#13) *3-4-96 at 8:30 PM (I had just left Linda's house and was approaching the corner at Hudson and Grant Street) – Craft passed over Linda's house approx. 25-30 ft. above heading east, passed over canal, then turned left and headed north (towards Cow Meadow Park) NO SOUND. Same flashing white strobes with red light in center bottom.*

#14) *3/4/96 at 10:58 PM – From rear door, saw same configuration of lights above area of fireman's field in industrial park (directly north of my house) turning left heading west over Atlantic Ave., near tower.*

3/25/96 – Had a UFO meeting at Linda's house. Caroline H. Joanne, Brian and Rick attended. Nuthin' happened. However, the next morning, 3/26/96 Linda noticed a red mark in her navel (there was three red dots in the shape of a triangle), which was irritating her. Same day – Linda noticed a triangular red mark on the back of my head, on the lower right side at the base of hairline. Same day, late afternoon, discovered scratch marks on the lower right and left sides of Linda's back. Right side marks look like "cat scratches" which are scabbed over.

On 3/26/96, I woke up to get my kids ready to school and I noticed that my bellybutton was itchy so I looked down at it and noticed three tiny pin sized red marks inside my bellybutton. [photo, fig. 2] I showed my mother, she was shocked. She reminded me that we had a UFO meeting the night before here at my house and wondered if something had happened that night after Joanne, Brian, Janet and Rick left. Later on that day, I asked my mother to scratch my back. She lifted my shirt and said, "Oh, my God. Do you know you have scratch marks on your back?" I said "What?" So, I went to the living room and used the mirrored wall to look at the scratches on my back. My mother and I have documented pictures. [photo, fig. 3]

#15) *3/29/96 7:38 PM – Hudson Ave., cor. of Jefferson St. – Saw very low craft come from behind building (north side of Jefferson Marina) level with the top of the 2 story building, heading SE over water. This craft seemed more round or disc shaped, very well lit up.*

Both grandsons witnessed craft at the same time (we were in the car) Bobby said, "Oh cool – an airplane real low." I told him it was no airplane!!

4/1/96 – I woke up at 2:45 AM and was wide-awake. I don't really remember anything happening before that. I went back to sleep. I told my mother about it later that morning and she said she woke up at 4:00 AM also wide-awake. Strange things are happening quite often lately. Mom has seen the triangular craft more frequently. I on the other hand, haven't seen any crafts for quite some time. I think the last craft I saw was with Ken (Sr.), while I was still pregnant, but the markings I've had were before and after pregnancy.

#16) *4/9/96 – at 5:35 AM – Had another fly-by, over rooftops across the street, east to west.*

4/9/96 – Regression therapy session with Dr. Jean Mundy.

4/23/96 – The Tower: This experience started as a gathering of several people almost in a party-like setting. We all were standing together near a building or tower. We were then invited by someone in the group to go ride in the tower. I do not recall who invited us. The top of the tower was rotating and the next thing I remember is being in a round room with a double row of seats all around this room. The seats were sunken into the floor in the dimly lit room. All around the room were windows and you could see that it was dark outside. What's funny is I can somehow see everything in this room from where I am standing. I was standing in the aisle next to a seat. I looked down and saw a couple seated. The male had his head tilted back as if he was preparing for take off or asleep. The female was a bit restless and said she wanted to open the window and was going to push the "F" button on the armrest to see if it worked. She was oblivious that the male sitting next to her wasn't paying attention to her. She pushed the button and immediately she fell through where the seat was and disappeared like a trap door. Her boyfriend didn't notice she disappeared. I immediately noticed a light blinking up by where the pilot was. There was a long control panel and when the woman fell through the red light started blinking on that control panel. This is when the man that was sitting next to her realizes his girlfriend is missing and starts to panic. There was a being standing at the control panel and I just knew he was the pilot or someone in charge, but he wasn't dressed like a pilot. There was one light blinking on the control panel and it corresponded to where her seat was.

The next thing I am aware of is that I'm floating outside of the tower. I can see the craft and the windows as I am floating in this bright golden yellow light. The texture of the craft looked like cement. Next thing I remember was opening my eyes in my bedroom and the alarm was going off. The clock read 7:19 AM.

#17) *4/24/96 at 9:15 PM – Craft came in from SE, over water, then over houses. Continued NW over industrial park, turned west, passed by tower and continued west. I had just gone outside to put the car in the garage; saw craft flying in as I was standing next to the car in the driveway...talk about being in the right place at the right time.*

4/24/96 at 7:15 AM – Woke up today as usual and went about my daily routine of feeding Jaclyn and getting the boys ready for school. I knew my mother would be arriving shortly so I also made a pot of coffee. She always came over to my house in the morning. She would stay with me all day and help me with the baby while I did my clients nails. After my morning routine was completed I sat down with my mother and had a cup of coffee at the dining room table. I noticed a slight pain on the back of my neck. When I placed my hand there to feel why I was in pain guess what I found. There was a long scabbed-over scratch at the nape of my neck (update: on December 1, 2017, I had the same scratch). [photos, figs. 4-5] I know it sounds fake or crazy. I think it sounds like I'm fabricating these things but they really happened to me. I took pictures of this scratch for documentation. Then as I'm getting my oldest son ready for bed at 9:00 PM that same day he tells me he had a dream last night of a flying top, like the toys that spin. It went spinning up into the clouds. He also said he saw two huge red eyes looking into his bedroom window. "They were mad," he said before the top went spinning off into the clouds. He's 8 years old. Did he go with me on the tower?

4/30/96 – Woke up at my usual time 7:15 AM to get the boys ready for school. Went into the bathroom and noticed a decent amount of rusty-brown blood on my underwear. I thought this was odd since I wasn't due for my period until May 6th or so. I put on a sanitary napkin and went on with my day.

5/3/96 at 7:15 AM – No blood today finally. Had two days of blood. However, I did notice that I had a scratch mark on my left hand on the top of my hand between my thumb and index finger. I also woke up feeling drugged.

5/6/96 – THE POOL – In this experience Jaclyn and I were at an outdoor pool. The water was very blue and the weather was perfect. I found myself talking with two other mothers while standing ankle deep in the pool. One woman asked me where my daughter was and I casually answered "oh, she's swimming" as I motioned with my arm towards my feet and down towards the water. Just as I looked down I saw Jaclyn swimming up to me under water. I went down under the water with her to swim with her. We looked at each other and smiled. That's when I realized we were both breathing under the water. It didn't feel weird at all it felt so natural. I put my hands under her arms and brought her up and out of the water. That is all I remember. Was this some sort of experiment? Was this really Jaclyn or her twin?

May 11, 1996 (there is #11 again) – My mother called me at work at the salon in Wantagh. I worked their part time on Saturdays. She called to tell me that my oldest son, Robert, woke up with his left nostril caked with dried blood. My mother also told me his bedroom window was covered up with his pillow. He and his brother slept in bunk beds and my oldest slept on the top bunk. There was one small window just by his bed. It was just big enough for his pillow to fit into the recessed area where the window was. My son told my mother he put the pillow there because the eyes were scaring him. Could the bloody nose mean that my son has an implant? I never had it checked by a doctor. I didn't want to know the truth.

6/24/96 – Ken's experience – This was the first time my husband (my ex-husband as of 2005) remembered an experience. He and I have had sightings before but this was the first time he was able to really remember anything in detail. Even though we've had several sightings in the past, he still remained somewhat of a skeptic until this. He was very animated as he recounted his experience to my mother and I. This is how his experience went. Ken and I were driving in his car and he saw something in the sky. It was a saucer shaped object that was brightly lit. He pulled over on the side of the road so I could see it better. He pointed it out to me, but I couldn't see it at first. Then as soon as I spotted it, it disappeared. Just as it disappeared Ken noticed that a woman was standing by his driver's side window. He could only see her head and shoulders. He said she was wearing a headpiece similar to a Nun's habit. Ken rolled down his window and he asked her if it was okay if we saw her ship. Just as he said that a beam of light was coming through the center of the car. The woman had disappeared just before the beam of light entered the car.

Ken said he and I went up through the beam of light and as we were ascending he felt a rush go through his body. The next thing he remembered was a strong urge to urinate and found a bathroom resembling one in a high school. As he was urinating a man entered and told Ken he had just seen a UFO. Ken said yes, he had just seen one also but didn't mention the woman with the headpiece on or the beam of light we just traveled through. Ken said the funny thing was that he noticed I wasn't around in or out of the bathroom. After we went up into the beam of light Ken said I seemed to have disappeared. I have no recollection of this experience at all. I wonder where I was taken to after we went up in this beam of light.

7/28/96 – The Passenger – In this experience I was seated in an airplane. I can feel the seat beneath me, I can feel the chairs next to me on either side and I can see all the other passengers entering the plane but the room feels round. Once we put our seatbelts on the plane takes off, but I cannot remember if we took off like a traditional plane or straight up like a helicopter. Just before taking off I remembered that there were no visible signs of any windows, just the seating area which was circular, not linear like a regular aircraft. But when we finally take off and are in the air I notice that to my left there is a window. When I look out the window I can see the runway and the airport we just left from. It was different though the area was unlike anything I've ever seen before. It was much smaller and more compact. There was one runway, one tower and one hangar. This whole airport was surrounded by mountains in a semi-circle. I drew a picture of it in my journal. I have scanned it into the book for you to see. [drawings and schematics, figs. 6-8]

UPDATE on 7/1/17 – I went to the Dulce Base in Dulce, New Mexico, for a UFO conference. Richard Smith was one of the speakers. Just prior to going there I did some research online about the base. There were photos online of the base and an artist rendering of the supposed underground facility there. I was shocked. The aerial photo on the internet and the artist's drawing of the tower looked just like what I had drawn in 1996. The artist's drawing of the base and the tower looked like the tower I mentioned in another experience in 1996. Seeing this online and then physically being there and seeing the mountain range only confirmed that I had been there twice in 1996. There was an eerie feeling that came over me the whole time I was in Dulce, New Mexico, in 2017. An overwhelming sense of déjà vu...

7/29/96 – Tarot Card readings – This was the night I had Joanne, my mother's UFO group friend and local psychic from Massapequa come to my house to do a tarot card reading for a group of friends. She did each person individually. When it was finally my turn she told me that I'd been flying a lot lately on a ship. Really...? For me that was confirmation of all the experiences I'd been having.

8/1/96 – My mother and I went to an Eyes of Learning meeting. We met up with Brian, Joanne, Janet and of course Rick. We were all meeting a new artist John Spears. Rick and I were very happy to see each other and were starting to have very strong feelings for each other. I am in love with him but I cannot openly admit it. It would change everything.

8/6/96 – The group came to my house for another meeting. I was very happy that Rick was coming over again.

August 96 (no exact date entered in my mother's journal). *Ruth's (and Linda's) "Possible UFO-related symptoms" in no particular order* (my mother Ruth wrote these down, some of these relate to me also).

* *Had a strong fear of going over bridges and water (and Linda) and of being on a boat, until late teens.*

* *INTENSE dislike of dentists (and Linda), syringes (needles) since childhood.*

* *Fear of early darkness in fall and winter, since childhood. One instance in childhood triggered this.*

* *Insisted on being awake and aware during childbirth (twice)*

* *Do NOT like to talk to people while they're wearing sunglasses.*

* *Hate to wear anything on my head. (and Linda)*

* *Wristwatches stop working on me; have for many years. (and Linda) (See Beyond My Wildest Dreams by Kim Carlsberg pg. 273)*

* *Had frequent upper respiratory infections as a child, especially around age 6-7. (Linda also)*

* *Had dreams of falling as a child. (So did Linda)*

* *Have had recurring dream of running, petrified through a big old house. (always the same)*

* *Had unexplained vaginal discharge, rust-colored which lasted 2-3 days around age 16-17. (see Secret Life by David Jacobs)*

* *Had one possible missing fetus, around 28-30 (also see Secret Life)*

* *Had irregular menstrual periods, starting at age 11 for three or four years.*

* *Do not like talking or performing in front of people (I quite taking piano lessons as a child to avoid a recital) See "Masquerade of Angels"*

by Karla Turner pg. 203 also Beyond My Wildest Dreams by Kim Carlsberg pg. 158

* Have had regular sightings since the end of 1994/beginning of 1995. Always seen at very close range all or most have been triangular shaped crafts with one possible exception.

* Discovered triangular mark on back of head, ear bottom of hairline close to right side of spine. 2/26/96. As of 9/16/96 I have two more triangular marks.

* Around March 1966, after staining for 3 days, had a "spontaneous abortion" (miscarriage) age 23 which surprised me because I had a regular menstrual period the month before, but the doctor said that the size of the fetus suggested I had been 2 months pregnant.

* Have had many, many phone calls – nobody on the other end, or I would hear a "click." (Linda also has heard strange static, garbled messages and clicks)

* Many phone calls, asking for a "Mrs. Garcia."

* Strong childhood fear of closet up at the top of the stairs in my grandmother's house. (She called it the attic) (I was paranoid about opening the door, I don't know why)

* There have been two instances of black, unmarked helicopters flying over the house – BOTH TIMES were on the two days when a UFO investigator was scheduled to be at my house. (separate days, a few weeks apart) (1995 early spring)

* Used to have red, itchy spot at the base of spine, which lasted quite a long time (years). It appeared for no apparent reason, and eventually disappeared just as mysteriously. (Linda has had two very itchy patches outside both ankles for years without any explanation)

9/5/96 – I put the boys to bed at 7:30 pm because there was school the next day. I sat on the couch in the living room just to make sure they went to sleep. I was close enough to tell them to go back to sleep if they got silly and giggly, like most kids fighting sleep. Since they were quiet, I closed my eyes and I instantly had a vision a control panel. I was awake, or so I thought. Could this be a downloaded message? I can vividly remember being told what each light represented and what all the symbols meant and how to position my hands to fly the ship. I could see in the monitor on the control panel that we were in space. I could see Earth in the monitor. How could this be? I was just in my living room.

When I got up to draw what I had just seen and what I was just told I couldn't remember any of it. I guess I wasn't supposed to write it down. I also know someone was with me giving me this information telepathically but I did not see anyone, just felt the presence of a being. P.S. the boys were watching an episode of "Are you Afraid of the Dark?" and it was about UFOs. The aliens were friendly and when visible they glowed just like the glowing feet I had seen as a child! I couldn't believe it.

8/31/96 – My mother and I went out east to the television studio where Joanne and Janet taped their Long Island T.V. show called "The Unexplained with Joanne and Janet." My mother and I were the guests for one of the tapings. We were being interviewed about our UFO experiences. Rick was there also taping a different episode along with some other woman named Elaine. I remember him sitting on the floor of the studio just off to my right about ten feet away off camera. This made me more nervous than I already was, knowing he was there.

11/3/96 – Ken (Sr.) my (ex) husband woke up at about 6:00 AM wide-awake but feeling sore in both upper arms. He remembers being consciously aware of pins and needles throughout his body before waking up. When he got up out of bed both of his arms were numb. He also remembers hearing a humming noise. My mother told me she woke up this morning with bruises and a scratch on her left forearm.

11/3/96 – Found marks on arms, small, round bruise and scratch in same area about 3" above wrist which had not been there the day before. Kenny (Linda's husband remembers an experience during the night of 11/2/96 – tingly numbness al over, hearing a humming sound and waking up with both upper arms hurting, as if he had been held down.

#18) *11/11/96 – approx. 6:00 PM (already dark) 18th sighting. Linda and I saw a UFO over area of Sr. Citizens housing on Mill Rd. and S. Main, heading NE; it was low and dropped even lower as we were watching.*

#19) *11/20/96 – 10:25 PM – I was looking out front kitchen window, watching Michele come in from her car; looked up to my left (SE) and saw "it" heading in SE Direction, it turned left (over water) and headed north! Michele saw it too! I asked her if she had gotten an escort home.*

11/25/96 – I was with mom holding a baby girl which I thought, at first, was my daughter Jaclyn. But when I looked closer it wasn't her. I said, "Who's my little alien baby?" She resembled my daughter but was

33

thinner, frail looking and had less hair. She looked like she was the same age as Jaclyn. My mother didn't seem affected by the fact that this baby wasn't Jaclyn.

#20) *11/28/96 – approx. 6:00 PM – Looked out kitchen window (west) saw bright "star somewhat low; not moving, looked again a couple of minutes later, to see "star" take off; it went south then turned SW over water (saw red light on bottom...)*

12/6/96 – 4:15 AM – The screen door was banging against the railing on the front porch from the wind and it woke me up. I got up opened the front door and pulled the screen door shut and went back to bed. The door started banging again, not sure how much time in between so I got up walked to the front door opened it to close the screen door when I looked up towards the sky and noticed four circles of lights in the sky. There was one large circle of lights on the left. All the lights were flashing like a strobe light and three circles of lights next to the large one. They were all flashing also. All the lights were white. The large circle broke up into individual lights and started dancing in the sky. That's when I felt something on my foot. I looked down and saw a very unusual bug on my foot. It resembled a cross between a frog and a grasshopper with red speckles. As I was looking at it the insect morphed into a man. That man turned out to be James the one who was at my house last year in 1995. He proceeded to hypnotize me and told me to go with him into a car that was parked one house away. I managed to escape his trance and ran back into my house. My phone rang. It was my (ex) husband Ken. We talked for a few minutes then I hung up and went back outside and back into a trance-like state. I snapped out of my trance only to find myself back in my bed and my alarm was going off. Weird...

12/15/96 – Lisa Kropp (Linda's high school friend and nail client) called, told me that "one night last week, about 3:30 or 4:00 AM" she woke up for some reason, and saw a bright light and noticed that her kids' swings were moving side to side in the yard for no apparent reason. (no wind was blowing) (The WGBB radio tower is practically in her backyard, and that is where the triangular ships flight path is)

12/17/96 – Neighbor down the block, Jennifer Vidas, told me she saw "pink" lights shining down onto her backyard "recently" on E. First Street.

12/30/96 – I woke up at 1:30 AM because I was very itchy. I went into the kitchen to take an allergy pill and went back to bed. At 2:00 AM I woke up in a severe panic and scared to death. I remember feeling pinned down and paralyzed. I couldn't move any part of my body but was aware of what was happening to me. My eyes were shut and I tried to open them but could not. I tried several times to get out of this grip to open my eyes and try to see something, anything. I managed to partially open my eyes only to see a very blurry and distorted view of a being standing by my dresser. I finally managed to yell "NO!" and that is when I snapped out of it at 2:00 AM in a panic. I turned to my (ex) husband and woke him up. My heart was pounding and I was so scared. I asked him to hold me. He rolled over and put his arm around me as I clung to him for comfort. I fell back to sleep but it was a very light sleep. I kept opening my eyes to check the room for any movement. I didn't feel safe after that. What an ugly and scary ending to the year. What happened and why was I so scared? Did I piss off these extraterrestrial beings?

CHAPTER FIVE
1997 - 1998

My niece, Melissa, came to live with me. I won't get into specifics but let's just say that her life wasn't the greatest where she had been living. Her father is my (ex) husband's older brother. Her mother abandoned her at age three. When she came to live with me she was nine years old and the Department of Children and Families was involved. I was asked if she could live with us by my father-in-law. I already had three children what was one more? I had to become her legal guardian in order to place her in the local elementary school. I went through all the legal hoops to become her legal guardian so I could register her for school. The Department of Children and Families had to come one last time to my house to make sure that she had a bed to sleep in, clothing and proper living conditions before they would close the case. Once they came and saw that I had provided everything she needed, they gave me full custody and closed the case.

As for UFO experiences, it seemed like it was a quiet year. There aren't any entries in my journal for 1997. I guess I was just too busy with my children and my nail clients. Here are a few from my mother's notes.

1/13/97 – Discovered thin red curved scratch mark on right side of abdomen, starting just above waist. (still there 2/10 and 2/21/97 but faint)

1/11/97 – (there's the 11 yet again) Linda had "episode" of numbness and inability to move while in bed. (same as 12/30/96)

2/3/97 – approx. 7:30 PM – Linda drove to my house, as she got out of the car, she looked up to NW, saw 2 "objects" flying one behind the other (rather high up) – same lights. (I saw them, so did Mike) heading NW

#21) 2/9//97 at 7:00 PM – at Linda's, saw craft come in over water,

heading north, low and slow, turned slightly NW.

2/19/97 – Linda discovered scratch mark (about 2" long) on her back, right side, just above bra line.

#22) *3/10/97 – approx. 7:15 PM – Saw light through living room window, heading north, over house – just before first (book club) meeting.*

5/4/97 – Linda and Ken saw a craft over wooded area, in Farmingdale (back streets) coming home from the bowling league, it was late in the evening. Saw same object week before, same area after coming home from bowling.

#23) *5/11/97 (11 again) – 10:15-ish – As we came home, Linda and I saw craft coming in over water (to the east of the house) low, slow and silent! Heading north/NW – looked out back door, saw it heading NW over Industrial Park, until out of sight. (Mike saw it too – he thought it was a "helicopter with a spotlight") but there was NO SOUND! (similar to #17)*

7/14/97 – Mon AM – Michele showed me four-five small bruises, two each on inner thighs and one Linda also has a small bruise on her right thigh, in a similar spot like her sister. (I saw it)

What's with the number 11 showing up all the time?

#24) *11/5/97 at 7:30 PM – From Guy Lombardo Ave (1 blk north of Merrick Rd.) saw a lit up craft heading NE, which slowly turned North/NW.*

11/9/97 – At Star People UFO meeting at Joanne's house, Michelle G. mentioned hearing a loud "bang" associated with her abductions – well... I have heard that sound several times in my life (usually wakes me up) which I have always attributed to "dreaming" but now I'm not so sure.

#25) *12/21/97 – 6:04 AM – From kitchen window saw lit craft flying SE, then SW (NO SOUND)*

1/29/98 – 8:30 AM – (woke up at 5:55 AM)

1) discovered (while taking a shower) a small, round bruise on upper right arm, the size of a pencil eraser.

2) Linda remembers an experience where she is arguing with a mantis-like being, shaking her fist at it saying, "why don't you let us remember?"

3) Have soreness (muscular) around rib cage area, esp. left side, (began to feel achy and sore at night) and back of neck. Wed. night – had smelled an acrid odor through an open window – same odor that I've smelled before.

4) 1/30/98 Friday afternoon the bruise had faded somewhat, and three small red "dots" showed on my arm in the shape of a triangle – what else? There were three solid red lines connecting the dots. Linda has had similar (but larger) marks, connected by raised welts on her right wrist bone [photo, fig. 9] and scratch marks on her left forearm. A couple of weeks ago, Melissa mentioned dreaming about 2 black dogs chasing her.

1/29/98 – This is my first memory of arguing with a mantis-like being. She was standing over me as I shook my fist at her. I was yelling at her and asking her why she wouldn't let us remember. Could this be the Crone that Rick talks about in his experiences he shares with us at the meetings?

2/15/98 (day of taping with Joanne and Janet) – Found small red dots in a triangle shape on right (inside) of forearm (later turned brownish)

2/20/98 – found same marking on left (inside) forearm, same size, more faded and "upside down," not to mention the triangular areas on my cheeks! (have been there for days... weeks?)

3/1/98 between midnight and 3:00 AM – Had a "dream" of being on a "ship" with another woman... Looked out the back "window," could see the ship was low to the ground, just coming in off water, going over what looked like a red brick or quarry tile dock or pier (?) which seemed to be just slightly under water – the "red" could have been a reflection of a light from another ship... I told the woman "We're on solid ground now," she seemed relieved. I was very much awake and alert in the "dream" – it seemed REAL!

April '98 – Have found several marks, on different days, in various places on my arms, chest and face – all triangular. Busy month! Kenny remembers vivid "dream" re: vertical tanks and see-though glass doors.

4/24/98 – approx. 6:00 PM – I asked my son Kenny if he could draw a picture of his experience for the UFO investigator. [drawing, fig. 10] He did and gave a very detailed story. He did not hesitate at all while telling the story and was not nervous at all talking to the investigator that came from LIUFON. My mother and I just sat there listening to him with our mouths open. His story is as follows: Kenny was beamed up onto a rectangular shaped ship. Robert his older brother, me, and Ken Sr. were already on board. My son Kenny said he was on the table and Robert, his father and I were in tanks that were filled with some sort of blue liquid. His brother, Robert, was removed from the tank and was allowed to stand next to the table and watch Kenny get examined. In the room with the tanks and the exam table was one alien being and a screen projecting another being. Kenny said he was the "captain" and spoke to the boys and the other alien in the room. Kenny described the alien in the room as friendly and would explain every procedure to him and Robert. The "captain" was mean. The alien was wearing some sort of brown bodysuit a something that resembled a red cape. He drew a great picture.

5/18/98 – Mon. PM – The marks continue; on legs now as well as arms, and face. Noticed a triangle on grandson Robert's right cheek today. Linda and Michele also have triangles on their faces. Have "rediscovered" old scoop marks on my legs, next to the shin bone (small indents) almost look like old scars. Mike has marks too; so do Robert and Kenny.

5/19/98 – Barbara H. (Linda's nail client) also has a triangular mark on cheeks.

8/20/98 – 11:15 PM – Saw a UFO over the house. Saw from bedroom window and living room window. Canal, Northbound, turned left, went towards tower.

1) The word "Reassurance" popped into my head.

2) Read "Angels on Earth" (guideposts booklet) on 8/21 or 8/22/98, pg. 31, had the word "Reassurance" twice on the page.

3) At T.V. Studio 8/23/98 working camera for Joanne, guest "Marilyn" mentioned word "Reassurance" during interview.

4) 8/23/98 PM – Read book "God Explains" by Bob Cecilio, saw the word "Reassurance" on pg. 64 (WHAT IS THE MESSAGE?)

CHAPTER SIX
1999

January 20, 1999 – I was given downloaded information. It was detailed information as to what is below the Sphinx. See my mother's hand written account of what I said in a somewhat trance-like state. It was if I were standing there, inside the building at the base of the Sphinx. I can still picture it vividly in my head.

1/20/99 – Description of outside, underground bldg. of Sphinx as dictated by Linda:

"Front has columns (pillars 6-8) Color of Bldg. – white pearlized covered porch, going to lobby. In lobby (foyer) constructed of solid white marble, shiny (no veins in marble) – floor, walls and ceiling. Columns in pentagram shape (as if seen from above); at foot of columns there are huge planters (in shape of scallop) – PLANTS ARE STILL LIVING – in distance (back wall of foyer) there are 3 (blue) archways (2 are recessed); center arch is doorway, doorway has two large blue doors. Tops of doors are curved to fit into archway. Lapis Lazuli Blue – extremely glossy."

January 29, 1999 – Jaclyn is three years old now and talks like a little adult. She chats constantly with, what I thought at first were her imaginary friends. Her siblings never did this, so I found it fascinating. She would babble at first but by the age three she spoke very well. So, one day my mother and I asked her who she was talking to. She replied in a very matter of fact tone. "They are my friends." There was more but I entered it in the final chapter under "Hybrid Twins."

My daughter went on to add a few more friends that she speaks to. "Raydus is the doctor. Yaydus is the teacher, he does many things for me and plays toys with me too." Then she threw in the monkey wrench. "Kaybee is my sister."

She is only three she's not old enough to know that I lost her twin. She was too young for me to explain that the extraterrestrials or the Elders were taking care of her sister up in the galaxy. She told me she had a sister! So, Jaclyn is my earthbound hybrid daughter and Kaybee is my hybrid star child. Yep! I'm going crazy.

10/14/99 – 10:00 PM – Triangular craft flew east to west, at tree top level across the street from my house, then turned southwest (at mid-block) and passed over Linda's house. (She saw it from back door).

10/15/99 – 5:30-5:52 AM (before sunrise) – There were eight separate sets of lights that flew overhead at approx. 1-2 minute intervals. Still dark, could not see shape, only lights. #6 looked slightly bigger, and more "round" because of lights. Looked as if they were gliding or floating along, at a relatively slow rate of speed. NO SOUND! Saw first set of lights fly over, north to south through far right window (bow window in kitchen) headed due south, then finally turned southwest. All seven others flew south, over area of houses across the street. Have seen this before several times over the last four years, but never so many in such a short time. Almost seemed like a scattered "convoy" all heading back to the barn before 6:00 AM – the magic hour. Could there be an underwater base, out there in the ocean, just off shore? Or, perhaps, a mother ship hovering over international waters, waiting for the little "cosmic taxis" to return? I don't think that planes would fly this way, so close together besides planes make noise! The left hand window was open, and being an early morning quiet neighborhood, there should have been lots of commotion overhead if they had been planes! (Neighbor on E. Bedell Street saw one Friday AM also)

10/19/99 – 5:30-5:53 AM – Saw four possibly five – same scenario. (neighbor across the street, said that it was a plane)

10/20/99 – approx. 9:00 PM – Saw a triangular craft going north as I left Linda's house.

11/14/99 – 5:37 AM – saw them fly over from NE to SW.

11/15/99 – Saw FIVE crafts at: 5:42 AM, then 5:43 AM, 5:46 AM, 5:48 AM, 5:52 AM

11/16/99 – Saw SIX crafts at: 5:22 AM, 5:25 AM, 5:40 AM, 5:56 AM, 5:50 AM, 6:03 AM

11/17/99 – Saw only 1 today at 5:25 AM

11/20/99 – Saw SEVEN crafts at: 5:26 AM, 5:33, 5:36, 5:39, 5:49,

5:51 and 5:57

11/21/99 – A little further west: SEVEN crafts at 5:29 AM, 5:30 AM, 5:38 AM, 5:49 AM, 5:53 AM, 5:56 AM, 6:03 AM

11/22/99 – Saw SEVEN crafts at: 5:31 AM, 5:33 AM, 5:35 AM, 5:36 AM, 5:45 AM, 5:52 AM, 5:56 AM

11/23/99 – BUSY MORNING! Saw NINE crafts at: 5:29 AM, 5:33 AM, 5:42 AM, 5:43 AM, 5:45 AM, 5:49 AM, 5:52 AM, 5:59 AM, 6:01

11/24/99 – Got up at 5:38 AM – ONE at 5:47 AM went right over my house! ONE at 5:55 AM over the house, a little higher.

11/25/99 – Didn't look – was sleeping

11/26/99 – Didn't look – RAIN!

11/27/99 – Got up at 6:00 AM - too late

11/28/99 – Got up at 5:15 AM. Saw SEVEN ships at: 5:34, 5:46, 5:48, 5:55, 5:57, 6:04, 6:07 – all went straight south.

11/29/99 – Got up at 5:00 AM. Saw FIVE at: 5:38, 5:45, 5:55, 6:00, 6:10 – all headed straight south.

11/30/99 – Nothin' Doin' – RAIN – OVERCAST!!

CHAPTER SEVEN

2000

4/1/00 – My mother was at my house as usual and asked me what was going on between Rick and I. At first, I acted like nothing was going on between us. Then she told me about the conversation Rick had with her. He had confessed to my mother how he felt about me, that he was in love with me. I'm sure I turned several shades of red. Shortly after that I was on the phone with him. Why did he have to tell my mother how he felt? I don't remember much of what was said over the phone. All I remember is the fight of all fights ensued.

6/20/00 – 12:45 PM – At Linda's house – "I got it" Linda said. Then she said the following: "Zep Tepi = Time Ship, the pyramid is a portal, an airport" "There is no time, time does not exist, it is used to transport from our time (dimension) to their time (dimension)" "Sphinx: location – visible landmark, beacon – dead center – to go anywhere else. That's why they were so interested in the position of the stars. Zep = "Time," Tepi – "First" – also: "The foremost point of a ship." She was almost in a trance-like state or channeling while talking. See book "The Message of the Sphinx" by Graham Hancock and Robert Bauval, pg. 206 re: meanings of "Zep Tepi and Linda's interpretation. See the "Yahweh Encounters" by Ann Madden Jones re: tabernacle; altar (Moses – Desert Sinai) Compare with "The Book of Truth" by H.C. Randall-Stevens re: similarity of altar under the Sphinx. [GOLD] (use of) (According to "Atlantis to the Latter Days" the being called Osiraes" is said to be the real name of Moses! Pg. 66-68

6/22/00 – 7:50 PM – Another "channeling" session with Linda at her house: "Blue Doors" First of Linda's recollections, in Jan. 1999, of what appears to be under Sphinx – see her drawings re: columns and color of three doors in room (under Sphinx) "Lapis Lazuli," (Linda and "The Book of Truth")

See pictures in "Atlantis to the Latter Days" by H.C. Randall-Stevens showing entrance and Temple under Sphinx. (Info was first "channeled" to author in 1925)

6/24/00 – Found more similarities – comparisons re: "temples" under Giza complex and Moses' tabernacle.

6/25/00 – In addition to being "Zep Tepi" the pyramids at Giza probably were the "center for mission control" for all the other pyramids scattered though out various key parts of the world. (see "Book of Truth" pg. 164, 166) (Also see "Keys of Enoch" by J.J. Hurtak)

7/3/00 – See "The Message of the Sphinx" by Graham Hancock, pg. 219, 163 – under sub-chapter heading "Searching for Horakhti" (passages from Pyramid Texts: these are probably flight path instructions for "pilots" or "astronauts" (not mystical mumbo jumbo); similar to what Sitchin describes in some of his "Earth Chronicles" books.

A five-month gap here... not sure why.

12/1/00 – Saw SEVEN at: 5:22 AM, 5:32, 5:34, 5:37, 5:39, 5:41, 5:50

12/2/00 – Got up at 6:00 AM – 6:19 (almost missed this one), 6:29 (much closer to house, lower in altitude and absolutely no sound! Turned slightly SW but not enough to make any approach to Kennedy. 9:08 AM saw small light silver plane fly same path as #2 should have heard engine noise but there was no sound!!

12/3/00 – Got up at 4:30 AM – 5:53 AM, 6:02 AM (close and low) both turned slightly SW, 6:09 AM, 6:14 AM overhead (NE – SW) very low; Michael saw it also, heard low "whooshing" sound but not typical plane engine noise; don't think it was a plane – even the small private planes don't go that low.

12/4/00 – Got up at 5:00 AM – "Star" in west sky, flickering more than usual (could see red. Saw SEVEN at: 5:48 AM, 5:51 AM, 5:53 AM, 5:58 AM (out of room 5 minutes) 6:09 AM, 6:20 AM 6:23 AM.

12/5/00 – Got up at 5:15 AM – Low, bet. Ed & Carl - Saw NINE at: 5:21 AM, 5:35 AM, 5:37 AM, 5:39 AM 5:51 AM, 5:53 AM and 5:55 AM were barely visible and distant, 6:03 AM, 6:07 AM.

12/6/00 – Got up at 5:15 AM – Saw SIX at: 5:30 AM, 5:34 AM, 5:44 AM, 5:57 AM, 6:02 AM, 6:09 AM. Around 5:48 AM, "star" dimmed to nothingness; but there are no clouds to block it!! I can barely see it, 6:04

AM – not visible – where did it go? And it's still dark outside...do starts turn off and on at will nowadays??

12/7/00 – Got up at 5:15 AM (no stars) no "convoy" traffic – just regular airplanes approaching Kennedy - ??? – sky somewhat overcast.

12/8/00 – Got up at 5:00 AM – overcast again, no stars...NOTHING!

12/9/00 – Got up at 5:30 AM – Clear with some lite clouds. "Star" is quite visible, flickering brightly, clouds keep obscuring it. Saw FOUR at: 5:41 AM, 6:08 AM, 6:18 AM, 6:24 AM – ALL SILENT, LOW AND CLOSER TO HOUSE (MORE EAST)

12/10/00 – Got up at 7:15 AM, TOO LATE!

12/11/00 – Got up at 5:00 AM – FOGGY, OVERCAST – NO SHOWS

12/12/00 – GOT UP AT 4:30 AM – Overcast – windy – had been raining – NADA!

12/13/00 – Got up at 5:34 AM – Clear – Full moon still shining. 5:37 AM overhead, 5:39 AM close, 5:46 AM a little higher and further away, 5:52 AM overhead, 5:55 AM NW to SE to S, 6:02 AM NW to SE to S, 6:05 AM NW to SE to S. No incoming planes during this time.

12/14/00 – Got up at 5:00 AM – RAIN...

12/15/00 – OOPS!! OVERSLEPT got up at 7:15 AM – TOO LATE

12/16/00 – Got up at 6:15 AM – too late

12/17/00 – Got up at 6:15 AM – WIND AND RAIN

12/18/00 – 5:15 AM – VERY WINDY!

12/19/00 – Got up at 5:11 AM – light airplane traffic. Saw SEVEN at:

5:50 AM, 5:52 AM, 5:54 AM, 5:57 AM, 5:59 AM, 5:59 AM, 6:03 AM

12/20/00 – 5:10 AM – SNOWING!!!

Nothing, not even airplanes

12/21/00 – Got up at 5:15 AM – Saw FIVE at: 5:45 AM, 5:56 AM, 5:58 AM 6:03 AM, 6:09 AM... didn't stay to look for any more.

12/22/00 – 5:15 AM – SNOWING AGAIN – NO "TRAFFIC"

12/23/00 – 5:17 AM – (CLEAR) MODERATE AIRPORT TRAFFIC – Saw SEVEN at: 5:35 AM, 5:36, AM, 5:41 AM, 5:52 AM, 6:12 AM, 6:20 AM AND 6:32 AM

12/24/00 – 7:05 AM TOO LATE

12/25/00 – 5:07 AM – CLEAR – Saw SEVEN at: 5:37 AM, 5:39 AM, 5:40 AM, 5:43 AM, 6:01 AM 6:27 AM, AND 6:33 AM

12/26/00 – Got up at 6:20 AM – Saw one at 6:46 AM was probably #7

12/27/00 – Up at 5:00 AM – Saw NINE at: 5:22 AM, 5:47 AM, 5:58 AM, 6:00 AM, 6:02AM 6:04 AM, 6:09 AM, 6:13 AM and 6:15 AM

12/28/00 – Up at 6:07 AM – Saw TWO 6:11 AM low and close, went towards Linda's, 6:31 AM

12/29/00 – Up at 5:55 AM – Saw SEVEN at: 6:06 AM, 6:12 AM, 6:23 AM, 6:26 AM, 6:28 AM 6:29 AM, 6:33 AM

12/30/00 – 6:15 AM – BIG SNOWSTORM!

12/31/00 – 7:05 AM – TOO LATE

CHAPTER EIGHT

2001

1/1/01 – NEW YEAR'S DAY – 6:29 AM – Saw TWO 6:37 AM and 6:50 AM

1/2/01 – Woke up at 5:18 AM – as of 5:52 AM – NOTHING!

1/3/01 – Woke up at 5:20 AM – Saw THREE at: 5:37 AM, 5:48 AM, 6:01 AM, 7:20 PM – directly overhead NW to SE towards Linda's house – was low and quiet.

1/4/01 – Woke up at 5:13 – As of 5:55 AM – NOTHING!

1/5/01 – Woke up at 5:25 AM – Saw SEVEN at: 5:37 AM, 5:46 AM, 5:51 AM, 5:53 AM, 5:55 AM and 6:03 AM

1/6/01 – Woke up at 7:42 AM – TOO LATE!

1/7/01 – Woke up at 6:24 AM – Only saw TWO: 6:37 AM, 6:43 AM

1/8/01 – Woke up at 5:10 AM – Michele and Jackie's birthday! Saw SEVEN (NE to SW close, almost overhead and silent!): 5:46 AM, 5:51 AM, 5:53 AM, 6:04 AM, 6:06 AM, 6:10 AM, 6:16 AM.

1/9/01 – Woke up at 5:25 AM – NOTHING, SNOW AGAIN!

1/10/01 – 5:00-ish AM – NO SHOW! 7:50 PM – westbound over canal, across the street – slow!!

1/11/01 – Woke up at 5:10 AM – Saw FOUR at: 5:31 AM, 5:44 AM, 5:47 AM, 5:52 AM

1/12/01 – Woke up at 5:10 AM – Fun and games time – Each one had a different flight path and different altitude… Saw TEN at: 5:27 AM, 5:31 AM (distant), 5:32 AM (overhead), 5:34 AM, 5:37 AM, 5:39 AM, 5:42 AM, 5:51 AM, 5:55 AM and 5:59 AM.

1/13/01 – Woke up at 5:18 AM – No other airplane traffic. Saw NINE at: 5:30 AM, 5:33 AM, 5:34 AM, 5:40 AM, 5:44 AM, 5:54 AM, 5:56 AM, 5:59 AM, 6:04 AM.

1/14/01 – Woke up at 5:42 AM – Maybe one or two – very distant – couldn't really tell – only saw red lights; plus very busy incoming airplane traffic.

1/15/01 – Woke up at 6:11 AM (Holiday) RAIN – OVERCAST – NO SHOW!!

1/16/01 – Woke up at 5:15 AM – OVERCAST – NOTHING!!

1/17/01 – Woke up at 5:26 AM – Busy Airport Traffic! But, saw NINE at: 5:32 AM, 5:34 AM, 5:35 AM, 5:48 AM, 5:50 AM, 5:54 AM, 5:56 AM, 6:00 AM, 6:03 AM.

1/18/01 – Woke up at 5:15 AM – (NO AIRPORT TRAFFIC) Saw TEN at: 5:26 AM, 5:38 AM, 5:41 AM, 5:48 AM, 5:49 AM Flew NW to SE over house into heavy clouds – couldn't see where they went. 5:55 AM east of my house, flew directly south, 5:57 AM same as #6, 5:59 AM same as 6 & 7 – NW to SE then turned south, 6:03 AM directly over house – went straight south, 6:20 AM west of here – directly south. #6-10 heard a low "rumbling" sound as they passed over the house.

1/19/01 – 5:00 AM – RAIN!!!!

1/20 and 1/21/01 – Didn't look – bad weather!

1/22/01 – Woke up at 4:30 AM – Saw SEVEN of them: 5:29 AM, 5:35 AM, 5:45 AM, 5:59 AM 6:01 AM, 6:02 AM, 6:10 AM.

1/23/01 – Woke up at 5:10 AM – NO INCOMING PLANES! Saw TEN of them: 5:32 AM – banked SW towards Linda's (a little closer than yesterday, over S. Main instead of Guy Lombardo) 5:35 AM Mid-block, 5:37 AM came NW to SE, over Edna's then south, 5:41 AM over Ed's (higher), 5:47 AM went SW 2 houses east of mine, 5:56 AM mid-block to SW to Linda's, 5:58 AM over Ed's went SW, 5:59 AM – NW to SE, turned SW, 6:01 AM over me, 6:04 AM directly overhead – only one with loud, low rumble again, went straight south (as if to say "That's all folks!"

1/24/01 – 6:10 AM – TOO LATE!

1/25/01 – Woke up at 5:09 AM – No Airplanes! EMPTY SKY – As of 5:52 AM – Somewhat overcast – snow flurries.

1/26/01 – Woke up at 5:10 AM – Distant over Guy Lombardo. Saw

NINE at: 5:26AM, 5:31AM, 5:32AM, 5:37(?), 5:38AM, 5:42AM 5:50AM, 5:53AM, 5:55AM, 6:07AM

1/27/01 – Woke up at 5:00AM – OVERCAST – SNOWING – NOTHING DOING

1/28/01 – Woke up at 5:46 AM – Clear; several incoming airplanes.

Saw the ships distant, over Guy Lombardo: 6:01AM, 6:21AM, 6:26AM, 6:28AM, 6:37AM got up too late, missed the first batch probably.

1/29/01 – Woke up at 4:45AM – (as of 5:32 NO PLANES!) Sightings: 5:39, 5:42, 5:51, 5:54, 5:56, 6:00 (all overhead), 6:03 (further west, over S. Main St.), 6:18 (mid-block) NO AIRPLANES!

1/30/01 – Woke up at 4:59AM – (clear so far) 5:15 two incoming planes. Sightings: 5:24? (over S. Main, turned – headed W/SW STRANGE!? Started raining at 5:52 – a few drops. As of 6:00 NO PLANES – NO NUTHIN! 6:07(went over Ed's, S/SW) – Sure, after I shut the camera OFF! (The only time I tried to a video camera – not too successful)

1/31/01 – Woke up at 4:46AM – Airplane traffic – 5:18AM. Sightings: 5:27 over Guy Lombardo, 5:30 Plane, 5:34, 5:35, 5:44 Plane, 5:48, 5:50, 5:52, 5:57, 6:02, 6:11

2/1/01 – Woke up at 4:56AM – Light airplane traffic at 5:30, no sightings just Kennedy traffic from the south.

2/2/01 – Woke up at 5:15AM – Somewhat cloudy; light airplane traffic. As of 6:03 – NOTHING!

2/3/01 – Woke up at 5:22AM – Light airplane traffic. Sightings: 5:31, 5:37, 5:38, 5:43, 5:51, 5:53, 6:07 (did flash, blink), 6:09

2/4/01 – Woke up at 7:42 – TOO LATE

2/5/01 – Woke up at 5:11AM – No storm yet, somewhat cloudy. No planes! Sightings:5:44, 5:46, 5:47, 5:51, 5:52, 6:01,6:03 – all went south 6:08 wind, getting stormy.

2/6/01 – Woke up at 5:21AM – Clear; plane traffic. NOTHING!

2/7/01 – Woke up at 5:19AM – Clear – Incoming Kennedy traffic times: 5:27, 5:29, 5:31, 5:34, 5:36, 5:38, 5:41, 5:44, 5:45, 5:48, 5:50, 5:52, 5:54, 5:56, 5:58, 6:03, 6:05, 6:07.

Sightings: 5:22, 5:33, 5:39, 5:40, 5:42, 5:45, 5:46, 5:57, 6:05.

2/8/01 – Woke up at 5:35AM – Clear – NO AIRPLANES – Saw 9 close by flying NW to SE at: 5:40, 5:42, 5:48 mid-block, straight south, 5:50 NW-SE, 5:52 higher up, 5:56 NW to SE, 6:04, 6:11 NW to SE, 6:14 distant

2/9/01 – Woke up at 5:15AM – Somewhat overcast – NO AIRPLANES! Saw 9 at: WOW!! 5:25AM (NE to SW – very low, overhead – "Big Mama") (low rumble sound), 5:31 NW to SE to SW, 5:33, 5:37, 5:41, 5:45, 5:51 low, mid-block NE to SW, 5:55, 6:02 east of house went south SW.

2/10/01 – Woke up at 5:33AM – Cloudy – NO PLANES! As of 6:10 – NOTHING!!

2/11/01 – Woke up at 5:09AM – Clear, regular light incoming traffic. Sightings: 5:20, 5:28, 5:41(distant), 5:43, 5:45, 6:02, 6:04*, 6:07, 6:09.

At the same time as I was watching #8 (*6:04AM), "Big Mama" (see 2/9/01) came VERY LOW over the house again (east to west, then NW). Heard that strange deep rumble – had to stand up to look outside, saw it on my side [of the street], then it crossed diagonally across the street, and continued over the houses, heading west. Then it turned NW at S. Main or just west of S. Main out of sight. (Was this #10?) Both days at least 9.

2/12/01 – Woke up at 4:18AM – Clear – NO AIRPLANES. Sightings: 5:19, 5:26, 5:29, 5:30, 5:32, 5:36, 5:53, 6:10, 6:12.

2/13/01 – Woke up at 5:30AM – Somewhat overcast, by 5:50 nothing happening, just airport traffic.

2/14/01 – Woke up at 5:10AM – Clear, light in/out traffic. Sightings: 5:19, 5:28, 5:31, 5:40, 5:44, 5:48, 6:00, 6:03, 6:07.

2/15/01 – Woke up at 5:15AM – partly cloudy; incoming plane traffic. 5:35 light rain – NOTHING!

2/16/01 – Woke up at 4:30AM – Clear – No Airplanes except for 1 outgoing plane at 5:32AM. Sightings: 5:17, 5:20 SW to Linda's, 5:28, 5:40, 5:43 NW to SE to S overhead, 5:47, 5:54, 5:58 straight south overhead, 6:06, 6:12.

2/17/01 – Woke up at 6:15AM – Clear; airplanes. Saw one at 6:12 (distant) probably missed the other nine.

2/18/01 – Woke up at 5:00AM – Clear; 5:25, 5:31, 5:37 HAD TO GO BACK TO BED WITH JACKIE.

2/19/01 – Woke up at 5:00AM – Clear – Just airplane traffic – NOTHING!

2/20/01 – Woke up at 5:15AM – Clear – No N/S traffic – just incoming from S, SE – lots of them.

*Note: Mike saw a triangular craft at 8:09PM, go diagonally over the house NE to SW NO SOUND!

2/21/01 – Woke up at 5:15AM – Just planes. PM – very heavy incoming airport traffic on either side.

2/22/01 – Woke up at 5:20AM – Saw 7, all mid-block heading SW: 5:30, 5:34, 5:37, 5:41, 5:44, 5:51, 5:55

2/24/01 – 5:22AM – Clear – No Airplanes until 6:02AM. Mid-block 5:36 SW, Overhead 5:41 S, 5:47 mid-block SW, 5:49 mid-block SW - Did I miss the first three?

2/25/01 – 6:45AM – RAIN!

2/26/01 – 5:18AM – ZERO!

2/27/01 – At Linda's – didn't see anything from Bobby's side bedroom window.

2/28/01 – 5:09AM – Cloudy – NO AIRPLANES UNTIL 5:52 – Cloud cover very heavy, just South of me, can't see far. AT 5:28 NE-SW overhead low rumble, 5:31 NW-SE-S over Ed's, 5:36 mid-block, 5:37 overhead heading south, low rumble, 5:46 overhead, low rumble, barely visible through clouds, #6 and #7 not seen, or at least not visible?

3/1/01 – 5:10AM – Clear – 5:32 SW overhead (passed in front of out-going plane, he must have seen it!!), 5:33 SW overhead, 5:46 mid-block SW, 5:54 SW over S. Main, 6:08 higher up overhead, almost missed it. PM – Plenty of airport traffic tonight – maybe A.M. will be quiet.

3/2/01 – 4:53AM – SNOWING!! – 0

3/3/01 – 6:47AM – TOO LATE

3/4/01 – 3/6/01 – SNOW!!

3/7/01 – 5:10AM – JUST AIRPLANES

3/8/01 – 6:08AM – TOO LATE

3/9/01 – 4:55AM – 4:57 – "Big Mama" again E/NE to SW first saw through east kitchen window, passed over Charlie's house next door then turned and went SW. 5:01 NE-SW close just east of house. Did I miss something, or just the last two?

3/10/01 – 6:48AM – TOO LATE

3/11/01 – 3/19/01 – either too late or the weather was poor, nothing was seen

3/21/01 – 5:00AM – 5:31 Came in VERY LOW, almost roof top level, then went LOWER after it passed my house behind houses across the street, somewhere closer to S. Main lost sight of it. – Could have been "Big Mama" again! 5:32 – right behind first one, a little higher.

3/22/01 – 4/2/01 – NO SIGHTINGS – either too late or weather was poor.

4/3/01 – 5:00AM – Clear (partly cloudy) The first one 5:14AM had more lights across back – flashed consecutively – "Big Mama"? was overhead and moved S/SW. 5:33 S/SW over S. Main Street, 5:34 5:38 5:40, 5:43, 5:47, 5:51, 5:52 - were all S/SW by S. Main Street, total time: 38 minutes

4/4/01 – 4:52Am – Clear – First one was mid-block and came from North to South at 5:17 – only saw one solid light, 5:29, 5:31 were S/SW by S. Main, 5:34 mid-block S/SW, 5:36, 5:37, 5:41, were S/SW by S. Main St, 5:44 was overhead N-S, 5:46 was overhead NW-E-SW, 5:49 overhead but higher, 5:51 overhead NW-E-SW (last 4 #8-11 hears slight low rumble as they passed over. WOW, WHAT A SHOW – ELEVEN!! Interesting, because there is also airplane traffic west to east but they are flying higher up.

4/5/01 – 5:01AM – Just airplanes – 0 – But, 8:48 PM – Just noticed two familiar triangular "objects" in the sky, heading south, @8:42 & 8:44, now another (3rd) at 8:49, banking right and heading SW as they always do in the AM, #4 8:53, #5 9:07 and #6 9:08 PM. If they are flying tonight, I probably won't see them in the AM...??? It is supposed to rain tomorrow.

4/6/01 – 5:03AM – 5:18 "Big Mama" overhead – heard it coming over from NE to SW with a low rumbling and "pulsating"; after is passed over Spencer's house I couldn't tell which direction it went because it was TOO LOW! (2) 5:28AM – NE-SW, (3) 5:29 – NE-SW, (4) 5:34 – NW-SE-S, (5) 5:37 mid-block N-S-SW, (6) 5:40 mid-block N-S-

SW, (7) 5:42 mid-block N-S-SW, (8) 5:45 mid-block (higher) N-S-SW

4/7/01 – 4/13/01 – BAD WEATHER – NO SIGHTINGS

4/14/01 – 5:50AM – Clear – Just planes (or did I miss them?) Linda's birthday 37

4/15/01 – 5:00AM – Clear (it's turning light outside) (1) 5:21 S/SW (2) 5:26 S-W-SW (3) 5:30 mid-block (4) 5:33 mid-block S/SW (5) 5:38 mid-block S/SW heard low rumbling – no red flashing light (6) 5:46 S/SW S. Main

*4/16/01 – 4:58AM – somewhat overcast, no sightings. * 9:17PM – from back door, saw first of four, LOW & SILENT, heading north over water, banked left then headed N/NW; all four within a 15 minute period. #3 and #4 very close together, saw from front and back windows. Haven't seen this in a long time!*

4/17/01 – 4/23/01 – NO SIGHTINGS

4/24/01 – 4:30AM – (1) 5:40 S. Main

4/25/01 – 4:44AM – (1) 5:38 S/SW (2) 5:42 S/SW

4/26/01 – 4:30AM – (1) 5:35 S/SW (2) 5:39 S/SW

4/27/01 – 12:17AM Couldn't sleep. (1) 12:20 S/SW/S

5/1/01 – 5:00AM – Clear (1) 5:16 N-S – Came in low and fast, then went lower so I couldn't see beyond the houses to tell what it was – only saw a couple of flashes of light, no sound.

6/9/01 – 9:50PM – Saw three triangular shaped lights headed S/SW (towards Linda's) between 9:50-9:52; "flight path" seemed to be over S. Main, too far to photograph.

6/10/01 – 5:30AM – Power outage till 7:00AM (power was already off when I got up at 5:30) Mike's watch was 2 hours slow.

6/11/01 – 7:00AM – Bobby (grandson) woke up with a nose bleed (again)

6/17/01 – I had moved with the kids and my (ex) husband to Florida. My parents and sister remained in Freeport, N.Y.

6/18/01 – found a small bruise on lower left arm; also needle puncture next to a vein just below elbow (area slightly swollen)

7/13/01 – One day during the week of June 25, 2001 pine needles were found on the floor of the car (front) on both the driver's and *passenger's side (more on passengers), under the hood (where it meets windshield), and stuck in the hinges of the driver side door. I have no idea how or when they got into the car! Yesterday, Betty saw them and saved some in a plastic bag. (she said, "Boy, you're weird." *Can't account for any missing time, nobody else used the car, no gasoline used excessively. **Check Dr. Brandel's parking lot for Pine trees.*

Some time after this entry my mother had a heart attack in my grandmother's living room and my father had to call 911. Thank God my father belonged to the Freeport Fire Department. They arrived quickly and resuscitated her. The way I found out was horrible. My father had left a message on my answering machine. My (ex) husband and I took the kids with us to go look at houses in Florida. When we returned I heard the message and started screaming and crying. I called my father immediately.

Near the end of August in 2001, my parents came down to Florida and stayed with me for a bit. One day, my mother came to me and said, "I feel weird." I said, "What do you mean you feel weird?" She really couldn't describe it, so I called 911, then I called my father who was out with my husband.

I waited until the ambulance left and had to rush to Jaclyn's school to pick her up then rushed over to the hospital. I can't remember if Jaclyn was with me or if I had someone watch her. What I do remember is getting to the emergency room and talking to the doctor who was attending my mother. He was going to have the ambulance return and send my mother over to the closest heart hospital. I followed the ambulance but had to pull over because I was having my first ever panic attack. When I got to the hospital the nurse who was attending to my mother came over to me and handed me a Xanax. I had never needed one before and started to tell her no when she said, "You are on such an adrenaline high right now, you need it. It will calm you down." I reluctantly took it. My mother had her aortic aneurysm repaired and came back to my house to recover.

The morning of September 11, 2001, I was coming home from dropping off Melissa and Kenny at middle school and I was listening to Y100 when I heard them say something about a plane and the twin towers. I thought to myself *'that's really not a funny joke.'* I really thought they were joking because they always are pulling some kind of gag on that radio station. When I walked into my house, my parents were sitting watching the local news. A plane had just hit one of the towers and, as we were watching the telecast, the second plane flew into the second tower. Wait a minute… what? I just watched a plane fly into the second tower! Holy shit, the radio station wasn't joking!

My mother recovered from that surgery and two more after that. One was to replace a valve and the second one was for an ascending aortic aneurysm. She recovered from them all. In 2003, my parents moved to Florida and bought a house very near mine. We hung out together as much as possible just like in Freeport. I was so happy to be with her every day again.

CHAPTER NINE

2005 - 2015

On August 23, 2005 I received a phone call from my father while I was at work. He said that my mother was sitting at the edge of the bed and saying things that didn't make sense. I asked what he meant and he said that my mother was saying that my boys were playing out front. I said, "Okay, ask her these three questions. What is her social security number, when is her birthday and who is the current president? If she can't answer them, she most likely is having a stroke." He asked her the three questions and told me she couldn't answer her social security or birthday and she said that the president was Ronald Reagan. Uh, okay Dad call 911 now. I will meet you at the hospital. I left work and met him at the closest hospital. As I walked into the cubicle where she was the doctor was also entering. I asked how she was doing and he was cautious with his reply. He told me that she did have a cerebral hemorrhage but it didn't look like it was still bleeding. So, she should be okay, right? He said no, maybe not. My mother was awake when I walked in to see her so I asked her the three questions again. She was able to answer them all perfectly. Ok, so maybe she would be okay. She closed her eyes after that. They brought her up to a room and put her on life support. I sat with her up in her room all alone and held her hand for quite some time. Her hand was still so warm but her body kept jumping. It was a bizarre thing to watch. I sat next to the bed holding her hand and put my head down on the bed. "Why, mom? Why...? Please don't go, I need you." I started crying and just laid there hoping for a miracle. I finally let go of her hand and quietly left the room and went home. I never went back to see her. The night my father, sister and my kids pulled the plug I wasn't there either. I stayed home with Jaclyn because I couldn't bring myself to be there for that. I still hate myself for not being there. On August 25, 2005, she passed away. That was the day that a piece of me died as well and I've never been the same since.

On 11/26/08, my son Kenny noticed three dots on the top of his left foot in the shape of a triangle. When he showed it to me, I decided to look to see if he had any other markings on him. He did. I found a red triangular mark on the back of his neck as well. Kenny has had several experiences over the past few years. He's had the paralysis on several occasions and they are usually followed by an experience that he tells me about the next day. Sadly, I never wrote them down. I didn't even write down any of my experiences.

10/1/15 – Woke up at 6:04 in a panic. I remembered the entire experience once I calmed down. This was the first time in a very long time that I was able to recall the entire experience afterwards. The following entry was my experience. I was in a classroom talking to two other women. We were discussing what we sensed or how we felt when we would see a UFO. That's when I noticed a huge rectangular UFO up in the clouds just outside this classroom window. Then from this rectangular ship out came a triangular shaped craft and it danced around the larger ship a bit. A strange feeling came over me as I glanced down towards the bushes by the classroom window. There were three small triangular UFOs hovering just by the window. As I noticed these crafts, I immediately started feeling numb and limp and then blacked out. I realized a few weeks later that the three small triangular crafts were there to take each of us up to the larger ship, one ship for each female in that classroom. I still wonder what they were doing with us. [drawing, fig. 11]

CHAPTER TEN

Somewhere In Time With Richard

On August 14, 2016, my life changed and my dreams came true! Richard called me out of the blue and confessed that he was still in love with me. He wanted to know if I would consider starting a relationship with him. Needless to say, I was completely stunned and after a few seconds of silence I finally spoke. He thought I had hung up on him or passed out. "Are you serious?" I asked as the tears started flowing down my cheeks! You see, for the past eight years I had been single and feeling sorry for myself, wondering if I was doomed to die alone. He was always in my heart and thoughts of him were on my mind continuously. He was someone I could never get out of my head and this one phone call was the beginning of something that we both had wanted ever since we first met twenty-two years ago. I knew it wasn't going to be easy. He was living in New Mexico and I was living in Florida renting a room in someone's house. We called each other daily and texted each other constantly. We had a lot to catch up on. For the first time, we could be open about our feelings and our relationship actually had a chance this time around. I remember someone asking me a few years earlier, I believe it was in 2011, if I would ever marry again and, after thinking about if for a few minutes, I said yes. If the right man came along, I most certainly would. Of course, the first person that I thought of was Rick but he was married at the time and living in New Mexico. I never thought we would be together again. We would just be friends and stay in contact via social media. Sometime in 2013, Rick called me and told me that he was getting divorced and was sad about it. I must admit, I was doing a happy dance inside my head. I didn't let him know I was happy about it, but I did hint that I would always be happy to be with him. I know I was being selfish but I had always hoped that one day we could be together. He kindly told me that he wasn't ready to be in a relationship with anyone in a text one night. Talk about being deflated.

I showed my cousin the text he sent me and she told me to just give it a rest. Leave him alone and stop pushing the subject. So, I did for what seemed to be an eternity. We did keep in touch via social media or a random text here and there over the years but it really wasn't what I wanted.

In August of 2013, I had an elevator accident at my job at Keiser University. My left arm was hurt badly causing me to have two surgeries and five procedures done to my elbow and wrist to try and fix the damage from the elevator door. I was fired from my job in 2014, one year after the accident. Their excuse was that I was taking too many days off from work and they needed someone "reliable." I was fired over the phone while at my doctor's office getting a new cast on my arm. Yes, the same arm that I had surgery on. Well, now I had no job and I couldn't afford to pay my rent. If not for the kindness of friends and family, I would have been left homeless. I lived with my son's girlfriend for quite a while, then ended up living with some strangers in their house for a few months with my cast up to my shoulder. Unable to work at that time, I was still recovering from the second surgery. All this took place from 2014 to 2015. In September of 2015, my oldest daughter Melissa came to visit me and after seeing the conditions I was living in, insisted I come live with her. So, from September 2015 to March 2016, I lived with her, her husband and their kids. It was a beautiful thing and I was able to fully recover while I was there. I finally got a job and was able to go back to work. Believe it or not, it was an old job I previously had in 2004 with the Broward County school district. Starting to get back on my feet, I eventually moved closer to my job and was renting a room in a house. This is where I was living when Rick called me that night to ask if I wanted to start a relationship with him.

In September of 2016, I flew to New Mexico to see him for the first time in eleven years. Yes, eleven. There it is again. I hadn't seen him since 2005, right before I got divorced, when he came to Florida to visit me. That was the very first time we were actually intimate. At the time, it wasn't exactly what we had imagined as it felt rushed and tense. I don't think either of us enjoyed ourselves. We had lost contact until 2009 when social media became the new trend. So, here I am in September, 2016, arriving at the Albuquerque airport. I went outside to wait for him at the passenger pick-up because he was coming straight from work. I sat there for a few minutes distracting myself by reading his new book. From the corner of my eye, I see a car pull up right in front of me. I just knew it was him!

I looked up and there he was standing next to his car staring at me with this huge smile on his face.

We ran towards each other and I was greeted with the best hug and kiss I had ever experienced in my life. We drove to his apartment where he already had a bottle of wine chilling. We drank that bottle of wine and ravaged each other with hot passionate sex like two people who were madly in love for years. We connected in such a magical and spiritual way that we knew this was truly meant to be. We had a fantastic weekend and on Sunday, when he drove me back to the airport, we both cried. I didn't want to leave and he didn't want me to go either. When I returned to Florida, we both decided the best thing would be for me to move to New Mexico and start a new life together. It wasn't an easy decision for me as it meant I had to leave my kids and grandkids in Florida. The only child of mine that wasn't in Florida was my second son, Kenny, who was married and living in North Dakota. Still, it wasn't easy for me to leave the state where most of my family was living. In December of 2016, I decided to surprise Rick and fly to see him for his birthday. I couldn't pull off the surprise so I had to tell him I was flying to see him. He picked me up again at the airport for another glorious weekend in New Mexico. It was on this particular weekend – Saturday evening – that he decided to turn the tables and surprise me. As we were eating the birthday dinner that I had cooked for him, he asked me to marry him! Yes, I know. We had only been dating since August of 2016 but we had such a long history and I didn't want to pass up this chance so of course I said yes. When I returned to Florida that Sunday, I immediately started to get the wheels turning for my big move. I asked my children what they thought and they all said that I should do it and live my life. They knew I was lonely, sad and depressed ever since 2014 when I lost everything. They said it would be different not having me near them but that I needed to follow my heart and do what made me happy. So, Rick and I came up with a plan on how to make the move to New Mexico and take the road trip together. He bought a one-way ticket to come to Florida in January of 2017 so that he could drive back to New Mexico with me and everything I could possibly cram into my Honda Civic. My poor trunk was ready to explode at any moment. But first, we had to stop in Tampa for something very important, Jaclyn's 21st birthday! Rick was glowing that day. He hadn't seen Jaclyn since she was nine years old and he was so happy to be there for such an important birthday.

The drive to New Mexico was long and scary for me, but we made it and as of January 12, 2017, I was living with Rick in his apartment. We got married a month later on Valentine's Day. A day I never thought would happen actually came true. In March of 2017, I was hired at an elementary school in the Albuquerque school district as the Principal's secretary. I love my job and I love the people I work with. As of mid-June, 2017, my son Kenny, who lived in North Dakota, moved to Albuquerque with his wife and son and made me so happy to have one of my children near me. If only I could get the rest of them to move here, that would be fantastic. In August, 2017, Richard and I purchased a home together! This is the first home he has ever owned and he says he only did it because he was doing it with me. He tells me all the time, "We are together now and everything will be okay. I am in love with you and I love you immensely." I cannot tell you how much I love my 6'2" Sasquatch but it wasn't always like this. You see, our story began twenty-two years ago on December 11, 1995, the day I met Richard Smith.

My mother had met him at a Star People meeting. He invited the entire group to attend his art exhibition at the Old Westbury campus for New York State University. My mother asked if I wanted to go with her, so I did. I was already very pregnant with my third child, Jaclyn, and needed a night out. We walked into this large open room and the first thing I noticed was this large piece of art hanging from the ceiling. It was lit up with these little light bulbs and resembled the frame-work of what I thought was a UFO. My mother noticed a group of people huddled by another art piece, saw Joanne was there and then said, "That must be him." As we were walking over to the group, I noticed a bunch of scattered copper pieces on the floor around the larger piece in the center. I saw another art piece centered in the middle of the floor in the next room, a large milk carton. Then I noticed him, the very tall red-haired guy in the room, the one that everyone was centered around in the huddle. "Hi, I'm Rick," he said as a hand was stretched out to shake mine. I smiled and shook his hand. Zap!! The electricity ran through me as our hands touched and our eyes locked on to each other like a tractor beam. Holy shit, it's him! I instantly knew it was him. Don't ask me how, I just knew this was the little red-haired boy from my childhood memories in my abductions. We didn't say anything to each other. It was as if we didn't have to. We both knew and we both felt it. Nothing else was said to each other that night. My mother and I left after we looked at all of his art, which included some fantastic paintings and sculpture pieces. During the entire ride home, all I could think about was this red-haired man I had just met and I wondered if I would ever see him again.

My mother and I went to Joanne's about a month after I had my daughter and there he was! I was so happy to see him sitting there. We glanced at each other and smiled. All we had to say to each other was "hi" but I could tell he wanted to say a lot more than that. I'm not sure when it happened but we exchanged numbers and started talking to each other more frequently, meeting at Pearl Art and Craft – in the parking lot – just to see each other. Eventually, it was to kiss each other but it never went past that. I felt too guilty because I was still married.

My marriage had started to go sour around the time I found out I was pregnant with Jaclyn in 1995. He wasn't too happy to hear that I was expecting again. Our two boys were eight and five and I think he was just fine with having two children. Now, here we are expecting a third one which is when he started acting distant and cold. Sigh, oh well. We went on with our relationship even though I was ready to move on by the time I met Rick. However, I was pregnant – very pregnant – so I stayed with him. At the time, I thought, "Why would Rick ever want to be with a pregnant woman? Who would want that anyway?" Now that I had Rick on the brain, being with my husband and pretending everything was okay was a lot easier. Rick and I became friends rather quickly. It was easy to be around him, as if we were old friends that were reunited and catching up on each other's lives. By 1998, I was working for the Freeport school district at the Junior High. On Saturdays, I was working in the S.P.A.C.E. program, a series of enrichment classes provided by the school district for the kids. Rick would meet me at the school almost every Saturday and would stay until I was finished. If he only knew how I felt inside about him. But I had to keep him at an arms length. I couldn't let him know how much I loved him. I was still married, on paper at least.

On April 1, 2001, Richard and I had a fight that completely destroyed our relationship. My mother was over my house and, out of the blue, she asked me what was going on with Richard and I. Boy, this caught me off guard. I had no clue why she was asking me this until she told me that Richard had confessed his feelings for me to her recently. Great! So, she asked me how I felt about him. At first, I said we were just friends but, honestly, my mother knew how I felt about him without me having to confess anything. She asked me if we had been intimate and I could honestly say that we never crossed that line. I wanted to but we never went there. I was so embarrassed about having to even have this conversation with my mother that I immediately called Rick. When he answered the phone, I ripped into him with such a fury that I don't think he knew what hit him. We were screaming at each other but what was really happening was an explosion of total frustration. We were both so frustrated at the situation we were in that it came out as a full blown no holds barred argument. The last thing I remember screaming into the phone was, "And, she's not your daughter!" Slamming the phone down, I hung up on him. A strong feeling of regret came over me instantly. All I wanted to do was run to him and tell him how I really felt about him, but I couldn't. I was a mother of four children and married.

In 2001, we moved to Florida and I had no contact with Richard until 2004. He was always on my mind and my marriage was pretty much over. So, late one night, I decided to call him at the New York Post. When he answered, I said, "Do you know who this is?" After his initial shock, we had a great conversation. He came to visit me in April of 2005, which was the first time we ever became intimate. It wasn't what I expected and I was a bit disappointed. I know he was too. It felt rushed and cold but I know it was because we had so much pent up anticipation from all the years past. When he returned to New York, we still kept in touch through email due to cell phone bills being very expensive. Calling long distance would have given me a huge bill. Things were not going well at home for Rick. His mother was very ill with cancer and he was busy taking care of her while lecturing. I was pressuring him during this time about returning to Florida to see me again and that didn't go over very well with him. I was being very selfish during this time. My marriage was a bust, my mother was also dealing with serious health issues and all I could think about was when was he coming back to visit me. We lost contact again and stopped speaking. I'm sure it was all my fault. I put too much pressure on him.

After my parents died, I was a total wreck and living with an alcoholic. We were together for three years and during that time I have no memory of any UFO experiences or any other memories for that matter. I was in such a deep depression that I have very limited memories from that period of my life. Things started to change for me in 2011 with a new job, a new apartment and a new car. My kids and I had a few good years up until my elevator accident in 2013. Then, in 2014, everything went to hell in a hand basket again when I lost that job. I was unable to work from the two surgeries and the series of casts I had to wear in between. So, I was forced to live in a room in my daughter-in-law's parent's home for about six months. Then I went to live in a home that belonged to hoarders for about three or four months until my daughter,

Melissa, came to visit me. That's when she saw the living conditions I was in and insisted I move in with her right away. By September, 2015, I was living with Melissa and her family and was finally able to recover in peace. In February, 2016, I landed my old job from 2001 at a Broward County middle school. I was thrilled to be back working with some fantastic people.

August 14, 2016, was when Rick called me and changed my life forever!

Over the past twenty-one years, Rick and I have had many discussions about our experiences and have come to realize that we share many similar memories of the experiences we had when we were children. We came to the conclusion that we grew up together on the same ship. When I met Gloria Hawker in 2017, I told her about my experiences and how I met Richard. She asked me if I knew what a love bite was. I said no, I had never heard that before. Gloria told me that it occurs when two people are paired by alien entities at a very young age. These pairings are kept in contact throughout their lives and most are made to have sexual encounters with each other starting at a very young age. After hearing about this, I started doing some research online. I did a "love bite" search on the internet and came across an article about Linda Cortile. She had a very similar experience as I and she had also been paired with a man named Richard. How bizarre is that?

Richard and I have had quite a few experiences together since we moved into our new home in August of 2017. We have explained them to Gloria and she suggested we go to her house so she could examine us with a special blue light she has used on other experiencers to see if we had any strange markings. We were not able to go to her home, so she brought the light to one of our New Mexico UFO and Paranormal meetings. Gloria was able to find several strange markings on our bodies that appeared as white marks when the blue light was used. She told us that this light was what Bud Hopkins had used with the people he was investigating.

I don't have any definitive answers yet and I still don't know what these alien beings want with me. However, I have this very strong knowing that we were chosen for something and that whatever it is, it's coming soon.

CHAPTER ELEVEN

Hybrid Twins

January 8, 1996, was the day she was born. All seven pounds, seven ounces and nineteen inches of her… and that red hair, hmmm.

Sometime in February, 1996, during an experience with an Elder [drawing, fig. 12], I was telepathically told this:

"This is your daughter. She will be kept here with us. You have been given permission to keep her sister on Earth. They have been chosen for a very special mission. The girls will be carefully guarded and mentored throughout their lives. They must be raised separately because it will be safer for them. In due time they will be called upon to work together. That is all you need to know now, but when the time is right we will give you more information."

"Um, excuse me?" I thought to myself. *"You are keeping one of my babies and not telling me exactly why?"* This must be some sort of bizarre dream, right? No, it wasn't a dream.

My daughter, Jaclyn, was a fantastic baby. She was always sweet, loving and happy. She seemed to reach every milestone easily, including teething. When it was time to start school, she fought us tooth and nail. She refused to get on the bus at first and continued to cry every day on the bus ride to school until second grade. There was some severe separation anxiety, I guess. However, learning was easy for her and, once she entered her classroom, she loved being in school. When she came home, she would play school with her dolls. By the time she was in third grade, she was already in gifted classes. I wish I could say the same about her twin but I know nothing of her. I was only allowed to see her a few times and I do not have any other memories of ever seeing her again.

Rick and I have been putting the pieces together regarding my pregnancy with Jaclyn as well. We firmly believe that Jaclyn is his child.

No, we have not done a DNA test to prove it because I don't feel the need to. I know what I know and that's it. And yes, my daughter knows about this. I've talked with her about it on two separate occasions and her response to this was complete acceptance. Somewhere between the latter half of 1998 and the earlier part of 1999, Rick remembers overhearing a phone conversation between both of our mothers, a discussion that centered around my daughter Jackie, Rick and myself. Part of that conversation had to do with a rather interesting photo of Jackie, a photo that left quite an impression on both of them and for a good reason. It was during this conversation that Rick remembers hearing his mother quietly say, "I find it quite interesting that she has that red hair. Where did that come from?" Of course, they both knew the answer already. Nothing more was ever said about this.

Jaclyn started talking to what I thought were imaginary friends when she was about one-and-a-half to two years old. At first, I thought it was cute because her older siblings never did this. She would have full conversations in her room alone. My mother and I finally asked her one day who she was talking to and, very matter of factly, she said, "Kaydus and Baydus." My mother shot me a look of complete shock with her mouth hung open. I couldn't show my daughter the shock I was feeling so I asked, "Who are Kaydus and Baydus?" She said they are her friends. She was about three at the time. My mother asked her to tell us about her friends, so she did. I honestly do not know how to spell these names so I am spelling them how I think they should be spelled. This is what she told us:

"Kaydus and Baydus. Kaydus is the little guy. He has a lidescope in his hands. He does science and math with me. I have to take a test. Baydus is a man. He does everything for me."

What?!? All my mother and I could do was stare at each other. She has had contact with them and they are always around her, watching her growth. This confirmed what my mother and I were told when she was only eleven months old (there's that 11 again!). The Elders were Jaclyn's guardians and have been keeping an eye on her.

In middle and high school, my daughter had all honors and advanced classes. She always had straight A's but every once in a while, she would get a B and freak out. She really didn't like getting any grade lower than an A. It wasn't something I forced upon her. It was what she wanted. I was never that studious in school. I was happy if I received a 76% as a grade in school. She was in the Honor Society, Mu Alpha Theta (MATH

Honor Society), and on the marksmanship team in the JROTC, a federal program sponsored by the United States Armed Forces in high schools across the United States. When she was sixteen, she had spinal surgery for scoliosis which she was diagnosed with at the age of fourteen. I didn't want her to have the surgery as I knew it was a risky procedure. Jaclyn was the one who pushed me to have the surgery done because she was in so much pain. She recovered rather quickly and has not suffered any set backs since the surgery. She made a YouTube video documenting her before and after scoliosis surgery and has had quite an impact on other young ladies who have had to have the same surgery. My daughter has two titanium rods and twelve screws in her back to this day. Her surgeon told us she could have them removed but the surgery to remove them would be riskier than putting them in. At Jaclyn's high school graduation ceremony, she received many awards. She went on to attend the University of Central Florida and completed her Associate's degree. She lives in Tampa with her boyfriend Justin and is now enrolled at the University of Tampa studying to become a nurse. She eventually plans on becoming a Nurse Practitioner.

She still has not had her awakening but I sense it will be happening very soon. Jaclyn is aware of her importance with the Sisterhood but has not shown any signs that she truly understands who she is to them. Rick and I will continue to support her and help her once that time comes. My hope is that one day she will be reunited with her twin and together they will realize their full potential.

APPENDIX OF IMAGES

Drawings, Illustrations & Photos

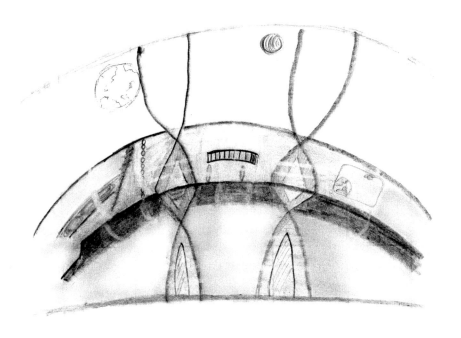

Figure 1

Drawing of the navigation console
I was operating on an alien spacecraft.

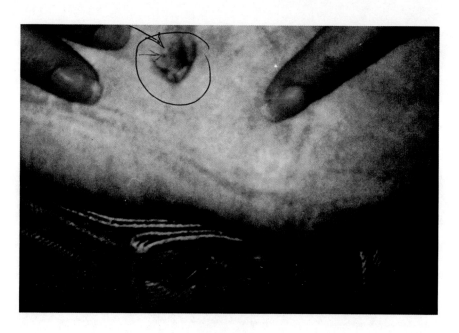

Figure 2

Photo of the pinholes in my bellybutton.

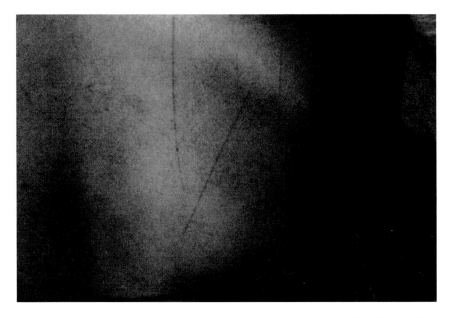

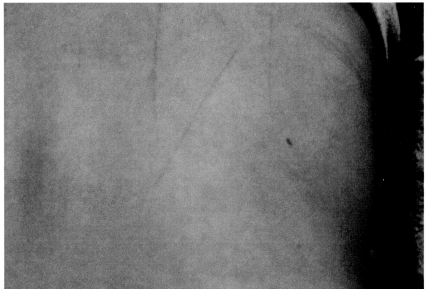

Figure 3

Photos of the scratch marks on my back.

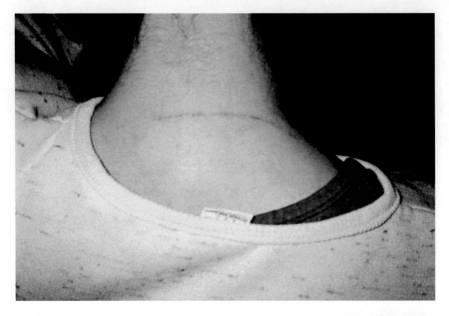

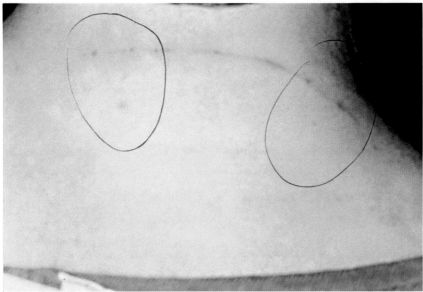

Figure 4

Photos of the scratch mark on the nape of my neck. Notice
the triangular shaped dots at either end of the scratch line.

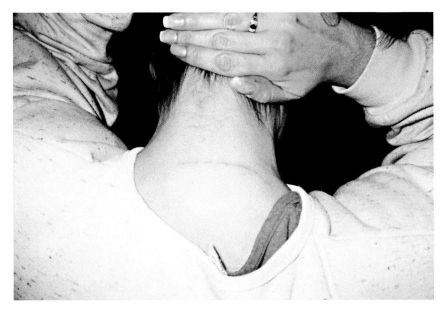

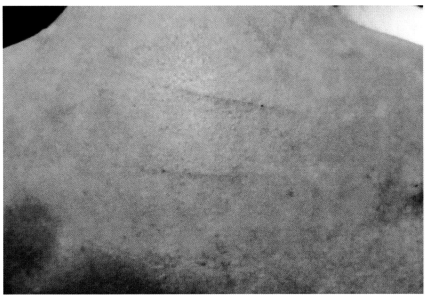

Figure 5

A photo comparison of the 1996 scratch mark on the nape of my neck
and a recent mark from December 1, 2017, comprised of three scratches.

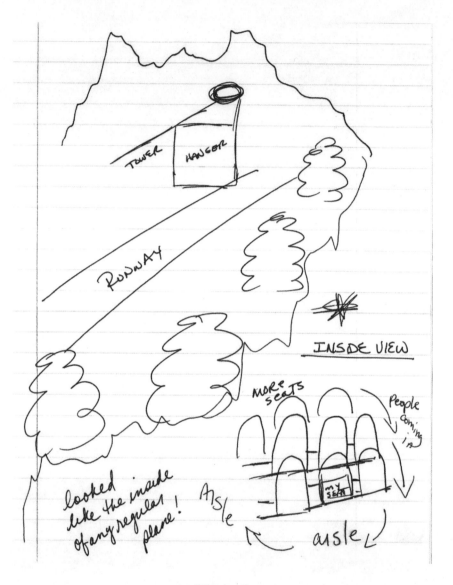

Figure 6

This is the drawing I did of my passenger experience.

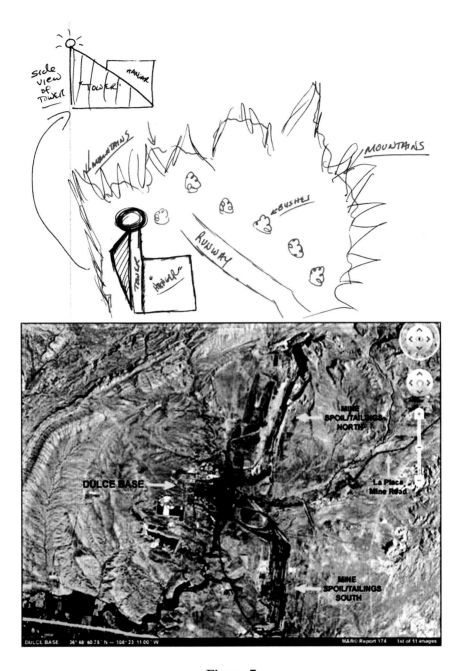

Figure 7

A drawing of my tower experience. I believe it's located at Dulce Base.

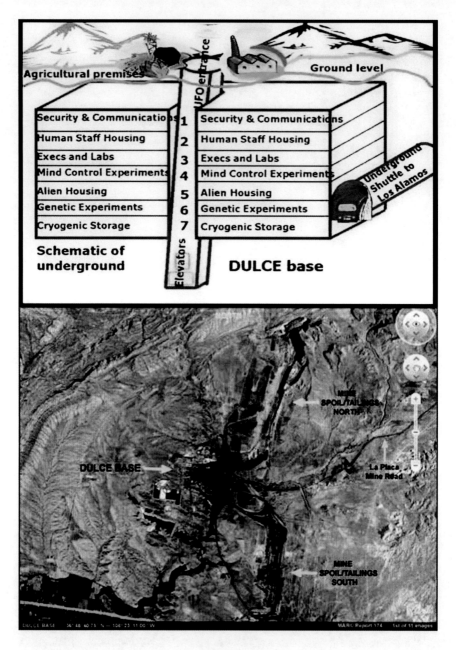

Figure 8

Here is a purported Dulce Base schematic I found in 2017
which is very similar to my own drawing of my tower experience.

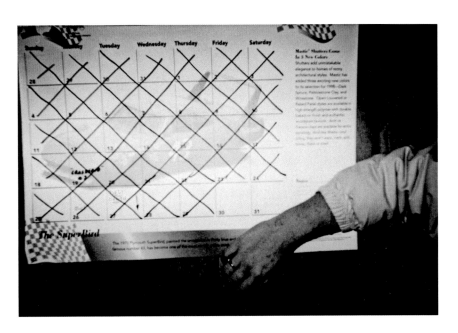

Figure 9

Photo of the marks on my wrist and hand.

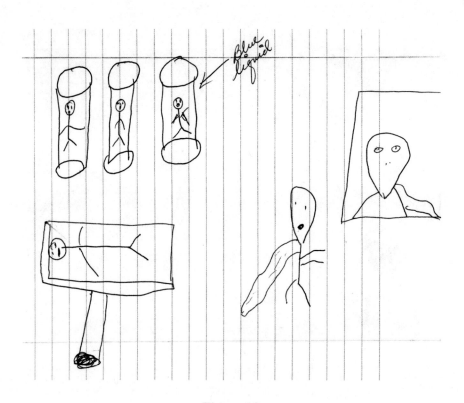

Figure 10

A drawing done by my youngest son Kenny of his experience.

Figure 11

A drawing of my classroom experience.

Figure 12

A drawing I did of one of the Elders.

Figure 13

An illustration of an undocumented experience I had that came out
during my most recent regression session with Gloria Hawker.

Bibliography

Angels on Earth Print Magazine. Harlan, IA: Guideposts Associates, Inc.

Bradbury, Ray. *Fahrenheit 451*. New York: Ballantine, 1953.

Carlsberg, Kim. *Beyond My Wildest Dreams: Diary Of A UFO Abductee*. Santa Fe, NM: Bear & Co., 1995.

Cecilio, Robert L. *God explains: All That Is, I Am*. Edited by Marilyn Wojtko Bruno. New York: Oneness Press, 1998.

Hancock, Graham, and Robert Bauval. *The Message of the Sphinx: A Quest for the Hidden Legacy of Mankind*. American ed. New York: Crown Publishers, 1996.

Hurtak, J. J. *Book of Knowledge: The Keys of Enoch*. Hardcovered. Academy for Future Science, 1996. A Teaching Given on Seven Levels To be read and Visualized in Preparation for the Brotherhood of Light To be delivered for the Quickening of the People of Light

Jacobs, David Michael, and John E. Mack. *Secret Life: Firsthand Documented Accounts of UFO Abductions*. New York: Simon & Schuster, 1993.

Jones, Ann Madden. *The Yahweh Encounters: Bible Astronauts, Ark Radiations and Temple Electronics*. 1st ed. Chapel Hill, NC: Sandbird Publishing Group, 1995.

Randall-Stevens, H. C. *The Book of Truth Or The Voice of Osiris*. 5th ed. Import. The Knights Templar Of Aquarius, 1956.

Randall-Stevens, H. C. *Atlantis To The Latter Days*. 3rd ed. Import. Channel Islands: Order of the Knights Templars of Aquarius, 1966.

Sky, Robert Morning. *The Terra Papers*. Phoenix, AZ: The Terra Papers.

Turner, Karla, Ted Rice, and Barbara Bartholic. *Masquerade Of Angels*. Roland, AR: Kelt Works, 1994.

Chicago/Turabian formatting by BibMe.org.

Index

About The Author

Linda Smith is a multigenerational experiencer for the past fifty years (spanning four generations), author and mother of four children. She was born in Manhattan, New York, in 1964. She and her family lived in Jackson Heights, Queens, until 1966, then grew up in Uniondale and Freeport, New York. She studied business at C.W. Post Campus. Linda Smith has worked in education since 1998.

Her maternal grandmother never really spoke about any experiences but did have an unexplained scoop mark on her leg since she was a child. Linda's mother always suspected that this was from alien contact but never asked her mother about it. Linda's mother, Ruth, started openly showing an interest in UFOs in 1994 and that is when she started logging every sighting and experience she had. Linda started journaling shortly after that at the request of her mother. All four of Linda's children have also had several experiences over the years. This makes them the fourth generation in this family having UFO experiences.

In September, 2017, Linda became a member of the Executive Council for the New Mexico UFO and Paranormal Forum. She is also a panel member for the abduction group for the NMUPF.

Linda has been asked to speak at the 2018 UFO Watchtower conference in Hooper, Colorado, and has been asked to be a guest several times for Aquarian Radio to speak about her experiences over the past fifty years. Linda and her husband Richard live in Rio Rancho, New Mexico, and are working on their latest project, the Human Origins Conference. To contact her for a speaking engagement, visit ufoteacher.com today.

Made in the USA
Monee, IL
20 September 2020